SANTA'S HOLIDAY TREATS

W·I·L·T·O·N
Wilton
ENTERPRISES

CHAPTER 1

HOLIDAY FOODS AND DESSERTS
4

Delectable appetizers and breads, irresistible sweet treats, dazzling candy boxes and bouquets to give. Here are Santa's secrets to easy entertaining with holiday sparkle!

CHAPTER 2

CHRISTMAS COOKIES
32

From elaborate spritz to easy caramel brownies, old-fashioned almond crescents to newfangled multi-color cutouts, it's the prettiest, tastiest selection of holiday cookies ever.

CHAPTER 3

GINGERBREAD
50

Wait till you see what Santa's done with gingerbread! Charming sleigh centerpieces, beautiful houses for beginners and pros—even gingerbread gifts like picture frames and ornaments. Our instructions, recipes and patterns make each project easy and fun.

CHAPTER 4

CAKE DECORATING
68

The grand finale to your holiday party—wonderful cakes in the season's favorite shapes. Discover delightful cupcake faces, petite angels and mini Santas that take just minutes. Or create holiday masterpieces like our yule log or wedding sleighride. Merry Christmas to all!

Here in our North Pole kitchen,
we're always making special
treats! Now, along with
Mrs. Claus and the elves, I'm
pleased to share some of our
most festive recipes and
decorating ideas with you.
Happy Baking!

Santa

CHAPTER 1

HOLIDAY FOODS AND DESSERTS

*It's the merriest time of year
to entertain! Count on these recipes
to fill your guests with
Christmas cheer: a savory multi-layered
sandwich loaf, delicious ham, cheese or
shrimp appetizers in fun
yule shapes, rich brownie-star sundaes,
jolly candy gifts and more.*

CHRISTMAS SANDWICH LOAF

Wilton Products:
Long Loaf Pan
Kelly Green, Christmas Red
*   Icing Colors*
Decorating Tips 3, 18
Disposable Decorating Bags

Bread:
3 Cups All-Purpose Flour,
    Divided
3 Cups Bread Flour, Divided
3 Tablespoons Sugar
2 Packages Rapid Rise Yeast
2 Teaspoons Salt
2 Cups Water
2 Tablespoons Butter or
    Margarine

Filling:
1 Package (5 oz.) Spreadable
    Brie Cheese
1 Package (4 oz.) Cream
    Cheese, Softened
Milk
5 Packages (4 oz. each) Goat
    Cheese, Softened
1 Large Cucumber, Peeled and
    Thinly Sliced
1 Jar (12 oz.) Roasted Red
    Peppers, Well Drained
    (reserve 1 piece for garnish)

Frosting:
4 Packages (8 oz. each)
    Cream Cheese, Softened
2 Tablespoons Milk

To Make Bread: In large bowl, combine 1¼ cups each all-purpose and bread flour, sugar, undissolved yeast and salt. Heat combined water and butter to 120°-130°F. Stir in ½ teaspoon green icing color. Gradually add liquid to flour mixture; beat 2 minutes at medium speed of electric mixer, scraping bowl often. Add enough remaining flour until mixture forms a soft dough. Knead on lightly floured surface until smooth and elastic, about 8-10 minutes. Cover dough and let rest on floured surface 10 minutes. Spray pan with non-stick vegetable pan spray. Form dough into a log shape to fit pan. Place in pan and let rise in warm place until doubled in volume, 30-60 minutes. Bake at 375°F for 30-35 minutes or until bread is lightly browned and sounds hollow when tapped. Cool on rack 10 minutes. Remove bread from pan and cool completely. Trim crust from bread on all sides. Slice horizontally into 5 slices.

To Make Filling and Assemble Loaf: Blend brie and cream cheese until smooth, adding small amount of milk if not of spreading consistency. Separately, stir goat cheese, adding small amount of milk if not of spreading consistency. Place bread slices on cutting board or counter. Reserve one fourth brie mixture. Spread top of three bread slices with remaining brie mixture. Reserve half of goat cheese; spread top of two bread slices with remaining goat cheese. To assemble sandwich, place one bread slice, brie side up, on serving plate or board cut to fit size of sandwich. Arrange half of cucumbers on bread; top with second bread slice, brie side down. Press together. Spread with half of remaining goat cheese; top with peppers and third bread slice, goat cheese side down. Press together. Spread top with remaining brie mixture. Top with remaining cucumbers and fourth bread slice, brie side down. Spread with remaining goat cheese and top with remaining peppers. Cover with remaining bread slice, goat cheese side down. When loaf is assembled, press firmly and refrigerate at least 1 hour.

To Frost: Mix cream cheese and milk. Frost loaf smooth with cream cheese (refrigerating sandwich before frosting makes it easier to handle). Tint any remaining cream cheese mixture with green and red icing color and place in disposable decorating bags. Pipe tip 18 rosette wreaths for top of loaf and tip 18 c-motion wreath border. Add tip 3 dot berries. Garnish with diced reserved roasted red pepper. Cover and refrigerate 3-4 hours or overnight before slicing.
Makes 16 entrée servings or 25 appetizer servings.

A party sandwich loaf is ideal to make when entertaining a large group. This Christmas version with cucumbers, roasted red peppers and upscale cheeses will be a show-stopping addition to your buffet table. Serve it as an entrée or an appetizer—just be sure to allow plenty of chilling time before serving so it will slice nicely.

Attention all Elves:
Santa's
Holiday Party

Saturday Evening
at the Workshop

This year Mrs.
Claus surprised me.
Her beautiful party cake
turned out to be a
delectable sandwich!

TREE APPETIZER TORTE

During the holidays many cooks stick to dishes that are traditional family favorites.
But when it comes to appetizers, hostesses are always looking for something unique and enticing.
This season intrigue your guests with an Italian-inspired cheese and pesto spread molded
in the Treeliteful Pan. It can be made up to two days before the party and
provides 25 generous appetizer servings.

Wilton Product:
Treeliteful Pan

Cheesecloth
4 pkgs. (8 oz. each) Cream
    Cheese, Softened
8 oz. Goat Cheese, Softened
15 Thin Slices Provolone
    Cheese (approx. ¾ lb.)
1¼ Cups Prepared Pesto
1 Cup Chopped, Drained
    Sun-dried Tomatoes
    Packed in Oil
½ Cup Pine Nuts, Toasted
Thinly Sliced French Bread,
    Toasted (brush with
    olive oil before toasting,
    if desired)

Wet a single layer of cheesecloth and squeeze dry. Line pan with cheesecloth,
allowing cloth to extend over sides. Beat cream cheese and goat cheese until
very creamy and smooth, about 5 minutes.   Layer ingredients in prepared pan
as follows:

> 2 cups cream cheese mixture
> 5 slices provolone
> ¾ cup pesto
> 5 slices provolone
> 1 cup cream cheese mixture
> Chopped sun-dried tomatoes
> Pine nuts
> 5 slices provolone
> ¾ cup (remaining) pesto
> 2 cups (remaining) cream cheese mixture

Fold hanging cheesecloth over top. Refrigerate several hours or overnight.
Unwrap top of mold. Unmold appetizer onto serving platter; remove cheesecloth.
Garnish with roasted red pepper circles and star, fresh basil leaves and additional
toasted pine nuts. Serve with toasted French bread slices.
Makes 25 appetizer-size servings.

Many molded appetizers, such as salmon mousse or spinach-cheese spread,
would be equally impressive on your buffet table if prepared in the Wilton Treeliteful Pan.

Expect friends to ask for this simple recipe!

Simple Party Fare

For hassle-free holiday entertaining, prepare these delicious appetizers in advance, supplement your menu with purchased food items and gratefully accept food gifts from thoughtful friends. Biscuit Boys and Cheese Reindeer can both be assembled or molded, then refrigerated several hours before guests arrive. Come party time, enlist your kids to help with the garnishing.

BISCUIT BOY HAM APPETIZERS

Wilton Product
Bite-Size Gingerbread Boy Pan

2 Cups All-Purpose Flour
1 Tablespoon Baking Powder
¼ Cup Vegetable Shortening
¼ Cup Butter

2 Tablespoons Chopped Fresh
  Basil or 2 Teaspoons Dried
  Basil Leaves
1 Teaspoon Mustard Seed
½ Teaspoon Dill Weed
¾ Cup Milk
Honey Mustard
Thinly Sliced Ham

Heat oven to 450°F. Spray pan with non-stick vegetable pan spray. In large bowl, combine flour and baking powder. Cut in shortening and butter with pastry blender or two knives until mixture resembles coarse crumbs. Add seasonings. Stir in milk until dough leaves sides of bowl and forms a ball. (Dough should be very moist. Add more milk if necessary.) Press 2-3 tablespoons dough into each cavity of prepared pan. Bake 10-15 minutes or until lightly browned. Cool 3-5 minutes. Remove from pan and cool completely. Cut in half horizontally with serrated knife; spread with mustard and fill with ham. Appetizers may be served cold or reheated and served warm. *Makes 18 appetizers.*

REINDEER CHEESE BITES

Wilton Product
Petite Christmas Tree Pan

Your Favorite Cheese Ball
  Recipe or Purchased
  Cheese Ball

Finely Chopped Nuts
Small Pretzels, Pitted Ripe
  Olives, Pimento for
  Garnish

Line pan cavities with plastic wrap. Form rounded tablespoonfuls of cheese mixture into balls; roll in nuts. Press into cavities; unmold. Garnish with pretzel pieces for antlers, chopped ripe olives for eyes and chopped pimento for nose. Serve with crackers.

Wilton bite-size and petite holiday pans are ideally sized for appetizers, snacks, muffins, cakes and brownies. Miniature treats are always appealing to children and the perfect size when someone wants just a nibble or a taste.

Don't spend your party fussing in the kitchen. These easy snacks let you enjoy time with your friends!

HOLIDAY ICE MOLD

Shrimp cocktail or crab claws look great in this icy star mold, on a bed of cranberries and pine. It's a great solution for keeping food well chilled during the party. As always, be aware of safe serving—keeping hot foods hot and cold foods cold for extended periods is essential.

Wilton Products:
Star Pan
Mini Star Pan

Water
Fresh Cranberries and Greens
Chilled Cooked Shrimp
Lemon Slices, Cut in Half

Fill large Star Pan with water to 1 inch depth; fill Mini Star Pan with water to ½ inch depth. Place on level surface in freezer; freeze solid. For large mold, place freezer-safe bowl on top of ice in center. Fill bowl with cans of frozen juice concentrate or packaged frozen food to prevent bowl from floating when mold is filled with water. Arrange berries and greens on ice around bowl. Add water to pan; freeze solid. For small mold, place metal measuring cup on ice in center. Fill with pie weights or clean marbles. Add water to pan; freeze solid.

When ready to unmold, empty bowl and measuring cup. Pour hot water into bowl and cup to loosen from ice; lift out. Dip pans in warm water to remove ice molds from pans. Return molds to freezer until ready to use. When ready to serve, arrange greens on waterproof serving tray with sides. Top with ice molds. Fill with shrimp and lemon.

These Star Pans, like many Wilton pans, are ideal for creating pretty ice rings or molds for party punches. Prepare large or miniature ice molds with water or ingredients from your punch and add fruits, such as strawberries, maraschino cherries and lemon, lime or orange slices.

MINIATURE QUICK BREADS

Co-workers, teachers and friends will love these delightful loaves as tasty coffee break treats. Or, tuck several loaves into a gift basket along with an assortment of jellies, jams and specialty teas. Since quick breads freeze so well, you can get a head start on the holidays by baking early in the season. The rolled fondant decorations make your gift loaves extra-special.

CHOCOLATE CRANBERRY LOAVES

Wilton Products:
6-Cavity Mini Loaf Pans
Ready-To-Use Rolled Fondant
Kelly Green Icing Color

1 Cup Sugar
1 Cup Vegetable Oil
3 Eggs
2 Squares (1 ounce each) Unsweetened Chocolate, Melted and Slightly Cooled
1½ Teaspoons Vanilla
2 Cups All-Purpose Flour
1½ Teaspoons Baking Powder
1½ Teaspoons Ground Cinnamon
¼ Teaspoon Ground Nutmeg
¼ Teaspoon Salt
½ Cup Dried Cranberries
⅓ Cup Mini Semi-Sweet Chocolate Chips

Preheat oven to 350°F. Spray cavities with non-stick vegetable pan spray. In large bowl, beat sugar, oil and eggs until thick and lemon colored. Beat in melted chocolate and vanilla. Add flour, baking powder, cinnamon, nutmeg and salt, mixing just until moistened. Stir in cranberries and chocolate chips. Divide batter among cavities. Bake 20-25 minutes or until toothpick inserted in centers comes out clean. Cool on rack 5 minutes. Turn loaves out of pan; cool thoroughly. Sprinkle with confectioners sugar. To decorate, tint portion of fondant green, leave remaining portion white. Roll out fondant following package directions. Cut tree and snow shapes for each loaf. Moisten back of shapes with small amount of water and position on loaf.
Makes 6 loaves.

CHRISTMAS
SURPRISE LOAVES

Wilton Products:
9-Cavity Petite Loaf Pans
Kelly Green Icing Color
Christmas Red Icing Color
Ready-To-Use Rolled Fondant
Ready-To-Use Decorator Icing

1⅓ Cups Sugar
4 Eggs
1 Cup Butter or Margarine, Melted
⅔ Cup Milk
1 Teaspoon Vanilla
2⅔ Cups Flour
2 Teaspoons Baking Powder
14 Fun Size (approx. 1" x 2") Candy Bars

Preheat oven to 350°F. Spray cavities with non-stick vegetable pan spray. In medium bowl, lightly beat sugar and eggs; beat in butter, milk, vanilla and icing color. Add flour and baking powder, mixing until smooth. Pour batter into cavities, filling one fourth full; place 1½ candy bars lengthwise down center of each loaf. Top candy with batter, filling each cavity half full. Bake 15-20 minutes or until loaves spring back when lightly touched. Cool on rack 5 minutes. Turn loaves out of pan; cool thoroughly. Heat Ready-To-Use Decorator Icing in disposable decorating bag in microwave at half power. Cut slit in end of bag and drizzle icing over loaf tops.

To decorate, tint portion of fondant red, leave remaining portion white. Roll separate ropes of white and red fondant; twist together to form candy canes. Moisten back of canes with small amount of water and position on loaf tops. *Makes 9 loaves.*

Holiday time is prime time for Wilton Loaf Pans in miniature and petite sizes. These quality multi-cavity pans are ideal for quantity preparation of individual nut breads, dinner loaves, snack cakes and appetizer patés.

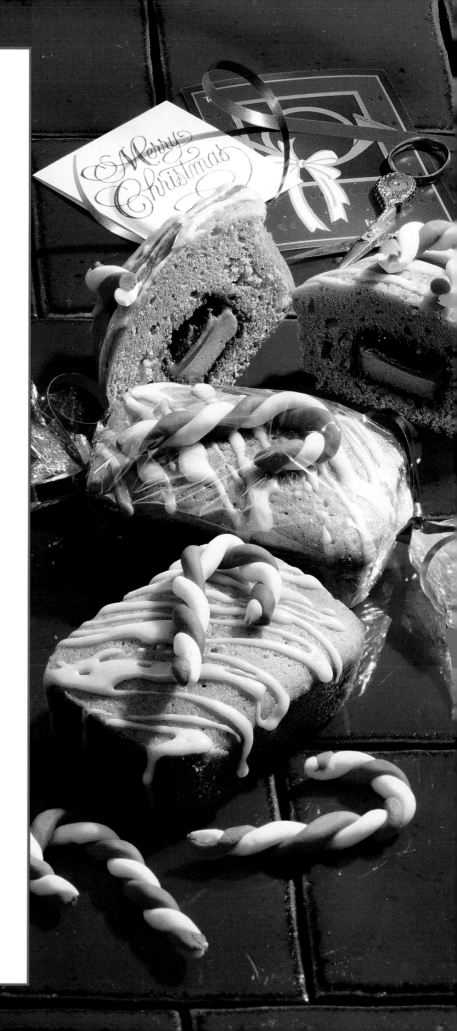

Holiday French Toast

Cooking with holiday flair doesn't have to be difficult—this easy dish proves the point. Baked French toast prepared in Christmas tree-shaped pans, warm maple syrup and fresh fruit make a satisfying breakfast on a cold winter morning.

Wilton Product:
Mini Christmas
   Tree Pan

Non-Stick Vegetable
   Pan Spray
1 (16 oz.) Round Loaf
   Hawaiian Bread*
2 Large Eggs
⅔ Cup Milk
1 Teaspoon Vanilla
Confectioners Sugar
Maple Syrup

*Available in most supermarkets. If unavailable, substitute other firm-textured bread. French toast is best when made with bread that is two to three days old.

Preheat oven to 425°F. Generously spray pan with non-stick vegetable pan spray. Remove excess spray from flat surface of pan with paper towel. (Do not use shortening or butter to grease pan; toast will stick.) Cut bread crosswise into ½ to ⅔ inch thick slices. Remove crust. Cut slices horizontally, rounding bottom edge, to approximate tree shape. Stir eggs, milk and vanilla extract together in shallow bowl. Dip bread slices in mixture; place in prepared pan. Press bread into pan with back of spoon. (French toast will puff as it bakes.) Bake 10-12 minutes. Cool 2-3 minutes. Loosen edges with small spatula; remove from pan. Sprinkle with confectioners sugar. Serve immediately with warmed syrup. *Makes 6-8 trees.*

Note: French toast can be made ahead. Refrigerate, covered, on cookie sheet; reheat in 400°F oven to serve. When refrigerated overnight and reheated, French toast trees will shrink slightly.

Cooks use Wilton pans, like the Mini Christmas Tree Pan, for every meal of the day. So why not wrap up a few as Christmas presents or economical grab-bag gifts?

After a long night of putting presents under the tree, this hot breakfast would hit the spot!

Apple Cranberry Pie

On a blustery winter day, fill your kitchen with the heavenly aromas of cinnamon, apples and cranberries.
Reindeer prance atop the crust, to show the delectable fruit inside. You can use the baked pastry cutouts
to garnish crumb-topped pies or as holiday snacks, topped with cinnamon and sugar.
Wilton cookie cutters make this an easy technique for any double-crust pie.

Wilton Products:
9 inch Pie Pan with Drip Rim
Reindeer Perimeter Cookie Cutter
Christmas Red and Leaf Green
*   Icing Colors*

1 Package (15 ounces) Refrigerated
   Pie Crusts
¼ Cup Butter
8-10 Granny Smith Apples, Peeled
   and Sliced
3 Cups Fresh Whole Cranberries
½ Cup Granulated Sugar
⅓ Cup All-Purpose Flour
¼ Cup Packed Light Brown Sugar
2 Tablespoons Brandy
1 Tablespoon Lemon Juice
2 Teaspoons Vanilla
1½ Teaspoons Ground Cinnamon

Preheat oven to 350°F. Line pie pan with one pie crust; prick with fork. Bake 10 minutes. Meanwhile, melt butter in large skillet. Add apples, cranberries, granulated sugar, flour, brown sugar, brandy, lemon juice, vanilla and cinnamon; cook until apples and cranberries are soft but not mushy, stirring often to coat apples and cranberries with butter mixture. Fill partially baked pie crust with apple mixture. Using reindeer cookie cutter, make cutouts on remaining crust; top pie with crust. Press edges together, clip with small scissors to make points; or press edges together with fork. Use small brush and icing colors thinned with water to add decorative designs. Bake 35-40 minutes or until filling is bubbly.
Makes 6-8 servings.

The Wilton 9 inch Pie Pan with Drip Rim helps you bake pies with less mess.
Its extra wide rim catches juices that can burn in your oven, and makes handling easier when removing baked pies.

Rudolph always
gets a kick out of
this pie!

CHOCOLATE FRUITCAKE

*All traditional fruitcake needed was chocolate! Baked in a fancy shape,
this jeweled holiday cake is studded with brandy-soaked fruits, chocolate chips and pecans.
Just one bite will turn your guests into fruitcake fans.*

Wilton Product:
10 inch Fancy Ring Mold Pan

1 Cup Candied Pineapple Chunks
½ Cup Halved Candied Red Cherries
½ Cup Halved Candied Green
   Cherries
2 Tablespoons Diced Candied
   Lemon Peel
1 Tablespoon Diced Candied Citron
½ Cup Brandy
9 Eggs
1½ Cups Packed Light
   Brown Sugar

1½ Teaspoons Vanilla
2¼ Cups All-Purpose Flour
3 Tablespoons Cocoa Powder
2¼ Teaspoons Baking Powder
½ Cup Coarsely Chopped Pecans
½ Cup Mini Semi-Sweet
   Chocolate Chips
2 Teaspoons Grated Fresh
   Orange Peel
1 Package (14 oz.) Wilton
   Candy Melts®* White

* brand confectionery coating

Preheat oven to 300°F. Spray pan with non-stick vegetable pan spray. In medium
bowl, combine pineapple, cherries, lemon peel, citron and brandy. In large bowl, beat
eggs with electric mixer until frothy. Slowly beat in sugar and vanilla until well blended.
Add flour, cocoa powder and baking powder, mixing well. Stir in fruit with brandy,
pecans, chocolate chips and orange peel. Mix until well blended. Pour into prepared
pan. Bake 65-70 minutes or until toothpick inserted in center comes out clean. Cool
on rack 10 minutes. Turn out of pan; cool completely. Melt white Candy Melts®
according to package directions. Spoon over top of cake. Garnish with candy clay
holly leaves and berries. *Makes 20 servings.*

CANDY CLAY
1 package (14 oz.) Wilton Candy Melts®, White
⅓ cup light corn syrup
Wilton Candy Colors Set

Melt candy as directed on package. Stir in corn syrup and mix only until blended.
Shape mixture into a 6 in. square on waxed paper and let set at room temperature until
dry. Wrap well and store at room temperature until needed. Modeling candy handles
best if hardened overnight.

Add candy color. Knead a small portion at a time. Candy will be very hard at start. If
it gets too soft, set aside at room temperature or refrigerate briefly. When rolling out
candy, sprinkle surface with cornstarch to prevent sticking. Thickness of rolled out
candy should be approximately ⅛ in. Cut leaves, using knife and your own pattern.
Use a toothpick to trace veins in leaves. Roll red berries between fingers. Dry leaves
over rounded surface for shape. This garnish can be made ahead of fruitcake.

*Bake beautiful, bunt-style cakes with the Fancy Ring Mold Pan
It's also ideal for molded salads and desserts.*

It's never too cold for ice cream—just add hot caramel!

BROWNIE STAR SUNDAES

The Wilton Mini Star Pan adds special sparkle to another heavenly dessert. Star-shaped fudgy brownies with vanilla ice cream and rich caramel topping is a delectable dessert that offers elegance with ease.

★

For casual get-togethers, make brownies in advance and freeze. Then assemble an assortment of ice creams, toppings, nuts and candies for make-your-own sundaes.

Wilton Product:
Mini Star Pan

2 Large Eggs
1 Cup Sugar
½ Cup Butter or Margarine
2 Ounces Unsweetened Chocolate
¾ Cup All-Purpose Flour
1 Teaspoon Vanilla
½ Teaspoon Salt
Vanilla Ice Cream
Caramel Topping
Chopped Nuts
Maraschino Cherries

Preheat oven to 325°F. Spray pan with non-stick vegetable pan spray. In medium mixing bowl, beat eggs; blend in sugar. Melt butter and chocolate in heavy saucepan over low heat or in microwave-safe container at Medium (50% power); stir. Blend chocolate mixture into sugar mixture. Add flour, vanilla and salt; stir (do not beat) until well mixed. Spread batter in prepared pan. Bake 15-20 minutes or until toothpick inserted in centers comes out clean (do not overbake). Cool brownies in pan 10 minutes on rack. Loosen stars at edge and turn out on rack to cool completely. To serve, top each brownie star with scoop of ice cream, caramel topping, nuts and a cherry. *Makes 6 servings.*

Your Mini Star pan also helps you celebrate many events from Memorial Day to Labor Day. Line with plastic wrap, fill cavities with vanilla frozen yogurt and freeze. Unmold stars and top with a combination of blueberries and sliced strawberries for a refreshing, light and very patriotic dessert.

Penguin Party

Our arctic antics will delight your guests as they serve themselves to delicious cakes and truffles. The penguins are easy and fun to figure pipe.

Wilton Products:
Mini Ball Pan
Sports Ball Pan Set
Tips 1, 2, 2A, 3, 4, 8, 12, 75
Black, Orange, &
Kelly Green Icing Colors
Candy Melts®*-2 pks. White
Creme Candy Filling Mix-4 pks.
Tree Former Set
Edible Glitter
Floating Tiers Cake Stand
Meringue Powder
Small Angled Spatula
Decorator Brush Set

Royal Icing (p. 78)
Buttercream Icing (p. 91)
Corn Starch
Corn Syrup
Granulated Sugar
Powdered Sugar
Shredded Coconut
Waxed Paper
Tea Strainer or Sifter
Christmas Ribbon

*brand confectionery coating

SUGAR MOLD RECIPE
4½ Cups Granulated Sugar
3 Tablespoons Water

Place sugar in large mixing bowl. Mix sugar so there are no lumps in it. Make a well in sugar, then add water. Rub mixture between your hands and knead for about 1 minute or until well-blended and mixture packs like wet sand. Be sure there are no lumps in mixture. NOTE: Keep sugar mixture covered with a damp cloth when not in use.

Igloo: Mix 2 batches of sugar following Sugar Mold Recipe. Dust each half of Sports Ball Pan with cornstarch to prevent sticking. Pack sugar mixture into each half, pressing firmly with heel of hand. Scrape a metal spatula at a 45° angle over pan halves to remove excess sugar. Unmold at once by placing cardboard circle over pans and turning upside down. To loosen, tap top of pan with spatula and carefully lift pan off. Use a thread, string, or metal spatula to saw ¾ in. off one side of each sugar mold for opening of igloo; to prevent cracking, do not remove the cut-off portion. Let dry for 2-2½ hours. Check to see that outside ¼ in. of mold has dried. Remove cut-off portion, turn sugar molds right side up and carefully hold in palm of hand. Do not squeeze or move sugar mold while it's in your hand or it will crack. Use a spoon to mark ¼ in. thick shell on inside rim of Sports Ball Pan molds. Start at center and gently scoop out soft sugar. After sugar is scooped out, smooth inside and opening of ball with your fingers. Place halves right side up on cardboard circle to finish drying for about 24 hours. Allow to cool to room temperature before touching. Make entryway: Place ring from pan on a waxed paper covered cardboard; pack ring with sugar mixture, remove ring, saw ½ in. off side; do not remove cut-off portion. Place a 2¼ in. diameter circle of plastic wrap on center to prevent center from drying. Let dry for 1 hour; remove cut-off portion, carefully scoop out opening, then dry 3 to 4 hours. Attach entryway to main section of igloo with tip 4 and royal icing.

Penguins: Figure pipe using royal icing. Using tip 3, pipe zigzag motion feet, overlapping at heel. Using heavy pressure, pipe tip 2A body to desired height; add tip 12 ball head. Pipe tip 3 tummy area and face, flatten with finger dipped in cornstarch or smooth with damp Decorator Brush. Tuck tip 8 into sides and, using heavy to light pressure, add pull-out wings. Add tip 2 pull-out beak, tip 1 dot eyes, tip 3 snowballs as desired. Make extras to allow for breakage and let dry.

Trees: Make 10-15 trees of various heights using royal icing. Cover Tree Formers with waxed paper, pipe tip 75 leaves. Thin icing with a small amount of water and pipe tip 3 icicles on trees. Sprinkle powdered sugar on trees using tea strainer. Let dry.

Snowball Truffles: Make candy centers following Filling Mix package directions, or use your favorite recipe. Roll into ¾ in.-1 in. balls. Dip in melted Candy Melts, tap gently to remove excess candy, then roll in coconut. Set on waxed paper to dry.

Mini Snowball Cakes: Thin buttercream icing with a small amount of light corn syrup. Spatula ice mini cakes fluffy, sprinkle with Wilton Edible Glitter.

Arrange *Igloos, Penguins, Trees, Snow Truffles* and *Snowball Cakes* on Floating Tiers Cake Stand. Add ribbon. Just before serving, using tip 4 and royal icing, pipe pull-out icicles along plate edge.

Save space on your buffet table with the Floating Tiers Cake Stand. Serve party spreads and breads, shrimp cocktail, dips, brunch muffins and more with dramatic flair on this elegant stand. Each tier will appear to float on air, especially when you decorate the branch with ribbon, tulle or garland.

My pudgy pals in tuxedos will make a splash at any holiday bash — formal or not!

NOËL BOUQUETS

SANTA'S WREATHS

Wilton Products:
Candy Melts®*—Lt. Cocoa, Yellow,
   White, Christmas Mix (Red & Green)
Red Crystal and Rainbow
   Nonpareil Sprinkle Decorations
8 in. Santa/Tree Lollipop Candy Mold
8 in. Lollipop Sticks
Decorator Brush Set, Candy Melting Plate
Parchment Triangles

Shredded Coconut

*brand confectionery coating

Melt candy following Candy Melts package directions and mold Santa Lollipops, set aside. To make four wreaths, combine 7 oz. (approx. 55 pieces) melted green Candy Melts and ⅔ cup shredded coconut. Trace circles on waxed paper measuring 3½ in. diameter with 1¾ in. center holes. Form wreaths and immediately add Sprinkle Decorations; let set. On waxed paper covered board, pipe free hand bows using a cut parchment bag and melted red candy. Let set. Carefully remove wreaths and bows. Attach bows to wreaths with melted candy. Position Santa Lollipop inside wreath and secure with melted candy. Package in Wilton Christmas Treat Bags for gifting.

RIBBON FANFARE

Wilton Products:
Christmas Lollipop Candy Mold
Candy Melts®*—Christmas Mix,
   Yellow, Lt. Cocoa, White
Decorator Brush Set,
   Candy Melting Plate
8 in. Lollipop Sticks

Holiday Container, ⅜ in. Wide
   Curling Ribbon, Ribbon Shredder,
   Gift Tinsel, Hot Glue Gun,
   Styrofoam Block

Mold an assortment of candy on Lollipop Sticks following Candy Melts package directions. You may cut 1-4 in. off ends of some sticks for ease in arranging. Wrap extra sticks in ribbon, secure with hot glue. To make loops, cut ribbon into 6 in. lengths; shred ribbon to within 1 in. of each end. Loop and hot glue crossed ribbon ends together. Wrap lollipop sticks with additional ribbon and glue loop to end. Cut remaining ribbon into 10-15 in. lengths and curl.

Fit styrofoam in container. Arrange lollipops and ribbon loop sticks by pushing stick ends into styrofoam. Add tinsel and curled ribbon.

CHRISTMAS EVE FLIGHT

Wilton Products:
Christmas Treats Cookie Cutter Set
North Pole Candy Mold
Candy Melts®—White, Lt. Cocoa,
   Yellow, Christmas Mix
8 in. Lollipop Sticks
Disposable Decorating Bags or
   Parchment Triangles
Fanci-Foil Wrap
Rainbow Nonpareils
   Sprinkle Decorations

Grandma's Gingerbread Recipe, p. 57
Styrofoam Block, Iridescent
   Shredded Cellophane

Cut four houses out of gingerbread dough; bake and cool. Melt candy following Candy Melts package directions and decorate cookies as follows: Fill in window areas with Yellow candy. Outline house details in Lt. Cocoa candy. Add wreath and bow using Red and Green candy. Add snow to roof using White candy, immediately add Rainbow Nonpareils Sprinkle Decorations; when set add White candy snow to window sill and at base of house. Use remaining melted candy to mold lollipops: nine reindeer (give one a red nose), one sleigh and one Santa.

Cut styrofoam into block 4¼ in. square x 2¾ in high, wrap with Fanci-Foil. Attach cookies to covered block with melted candy. Arrange lollipops in block by pushing in stick ends at angles shown. Add shredded cellophane.

If it reminds you of Christmas, it's here on a Wilton candy mold.
You'll find dozens of beautifully detailed designs in our
multi-shape sets. And if you're looking for great ways to use
Wilton candy molds, check out the Wilton Candy Easy as 1-2-3 Book.

Here's a great gift you won't find in a store!

SEASON'S GREETINGS

Star Bright Candy Boxes

Here is a great take-home gift for your party guests. Molding both the shells and the candies inside is so easy—and you can use any Wilton Christmas Mold to create your favorite seasonal shapes.

Wilton Products:
Mini Star Pan
Christmas Candy Molds (North Pole, Santa/Tree and Christmas Lollipop molds used here)
Tip 2
Light Cocoa, Yellow, White, Christmas Mix Candy Melts®*
Candy Melting Plate, Decorator Brush Set
Disposable Decorating Bags

*brand confectionery coating

Note: For melting directions, refer to the back of the Candy Melts package.

Mold candy shells using Mini Star Pan and melted Candy Melts, following either of these methods: fill molds with candy, let chill in refrigerator for 10-15 minutes or until a ¼ in. shell has formed. Pour out excess candy, smooth top edges with spatula and chill for 15-20 minutes longer. Or coat pan, one layer at a time, with melted candy, cooling in refrigerator between each layer. Carefully unmold shells by gripping inside of shell with thumbs and easing up and out. Decorate tops and bottoms separately, using melted candy in Disposable Bag fitted with tip 2: Pipe dot and bead borders and accents, print names, pipe dot and zigzag garlands. Let set.

Mold additional candy for box, following instructions for "painting" and "layering" methods on mold packages or in Wilton Candy Easy As 1-2-3 book. (Use Candy Melting Plate and Decorator Brushes for painting.) Refrigerate until set; unmold. Position candy in bottom shells or at center of some top shells, attaching with melted candy.

With Wilton Candy Melts, you'll create decorative candies that are colorful, flavorful and perfect for the holidays. Candy Melts melt smooth and fast in your microwave or a double boiler—they're as easy for decorating as icing. You'll find Candy Melts in Christmas colors at your Wilton dealer.

JILL

Good things
come in spectacular
packages!

CHAPTER 2

CHRISTMAS COOKIES

New flavors and cool colors make
a joyful holiday tradition even more fun!
And check out our great cookie gifts:
decorated cards, 3-D centerpieces and cookie pops
in favorite Christmas shapes.

COOKIE EXCHANGE

*Hosting a cookie exchange will make holiday baking easier and you'll have a great
selection of treats to munch on during the holidays. Here are two types of cookies to swap with friends.
The Peppermint Candy Cane Cookies add a pretty shape to your cookie platter. Christmas Caramel
Brownies are quick-to-make bar cookies embellished with piped Candy Melts. Put on
the carols, and water for tea, then enjoy.*

CANDY CANE COOKIES

Wilton Products:
Cookie Sheets
Cooling Grid
Pink Icing Color

Roll-Out Cookie
  Recipe (p.40)
½ Teaspoon Peppermint
  Extract (added to
  cookie dough)

Divide Roll-Out Cookie Dough in half. Tint one half pink. Roll a small piece of
pink dough and a small piece white dough separately into 6 in. logs. Twist and
bend into a rope candy cane shape. Place on ungreased cookie sheet, bake 10
minutes or until edges just begin to brown. Remove and cool on rack.
Makes 2 dozen.

CHRISTMAS CARAMEL BROWNIES

Wilton Products:
9 x 13 in. Sheet Pan
Cooling Grid
Pink Candy Melts
  (1 bag needed)
Disposable Decorating Bags

1 Cup Butter or Margarine,
  Softened
1 Cup Granulated Sugar
½ Cup Packed Brown Sugar
4 Ounces (4 squares)
  Unsweetened Chocolate,
  Melted
2 Eggs, Lightly Beaten
1 Teaspoon Vanilla
1½ Cups Flour
1 Teaspoon Baking Soda
1 Cup Semi-sweet Chocolate
  Chips
½ Cup Chopped Pecans,
  Toasted
½ Cup Almond Brickle Chips
½ Cup Caramel Ice Cream
  Topping, Divided

Preheat oven to 350°F. Line pan with aluminum foil, leaving 1-inch overhang at
each end. Combine butter and sugars in large bowl; beat until smooth and
creamy. Stir in melted chocolate, eggs and vanilla. Mix flour and baking soda;
add to creamed mixture. Stir just until combined. Add chocolate chips, pecans,
brickle chips and ¼ cup caramel topping. Spread batter into prepared pan. Top
with remaining caramel topping; lightly run small metal spatula across surface to
incorporate topping into batter. Bake 35-40 minutes or until toothpick inserted
in center comes out clean. Cool on rack; sprinkle with additional confectioners
sugar. Cut into 1½ in. squares or wrap in foil and freeze. Using melted Candy
Melts and a cut disposable bag, pipe decorative shapes on top of brownies.
Makes about 4 dozen brownies.

*When baking cookies, it's important to place dough on cool cookie sheets so cookies won't
spread before baking. Having two or more versatile Wilton cookie sheets and pans in your
bakeware collection is a real convenience.*

These are the cookies I like to see when I've come down the chimney!

CRANBERRY COOKIES

Wilton Product:
Petite Christmas Tree Pan

1 Cup Butter, Softened
1 Cup Sugar
2 Eggs
1½ Teaspoons Vanilla
½ Teaspoon Dried or
  1 Teaspoon Fresh Grated
  Lemon Peel
2¼ Cups Flour
½ Cup Quick Cooking Oats
1½ Teaspoons Baking Powder
½ Teaspoon Salt
½ Cup Dried Cranberries or
  ½ Cup Fresh Cranberries, Chopped
Buttercream Icing (p. 91)

Preheat oven to 350°F. Spray pan with non-stick vegetable pan spray. In medium bowl, cream butter and sugar. Beat in eggs, vanilla and peel. In second bowl, combine all dry ingredients except cranberries. Add to butter mixture and stir just until combined. Stir in cranberries. Press dough into prepared pan, filling each cavity half full. Bake 6-8 minutes or until lightly browned around edges. Cool in pan on rack 5 minutes. Turn out onto cooling grid; cool completely. Drizzle with icing; garnish with additional dried cranberries, if desired. *Makes 2-3 dozen.*

DIFFERENT DRUMS

Wilton Products:
Round Nesting Cookie Cutter Set
Christmas Red, Kelly Green,
  Golden Yellow Icing Colors
Cookie Sheets
Tips 2, 3

Roll-Out Cookie Dough (p. 40)
Snow White Buttercream Icing (below)
Miniature Marshmallows
Red String Licorice

Note: Regular buttercream can be used, however the icing will remain slightly soft.

Using dough for Roll-Out Cookies and 2 in. round cutter, cut out and bake 3 cookies for each drum. Cool on rack. Using Buttercream Icing, sandwich 3 cookies together; ice sides smooth. (Do not ice tops.) Pipe tip 3 top and bottom bead borders. Divide drum into 8ths and pipe tip 3 dots at top division marks; pipe dots at bottom border, placed between those on top. Connect dots, alternating from top to bottom, with tip 2 strings. Push licorice into marshmallows to form drum mallets.
Makes 7-8 drums.

ALMOND CRESCENTS

Wilton Product:
Cookie Sheets

1 Cup Butter, Softened
½ Cup Granulated Sugar
½ Cup Confectioners Sugar
1 Egg
1 Tablespoon Vanilla
2½ - 3 Cups Flour
1 Teaspoon Baking Powder
¼ Teaspoon Salt
½ Cup Toasted Slivered
  Almonds, Ground
Confectioners Sugar

Preheat oven to 350°F. In large bowl, cream butter, granulated sugar and ½ cup confectioners sugar. Add egg and vanilla. Stir in 2½ cups flour, baking powder and salt. Add ground almonds. Mix thoroughly to form a stiff dough, adding additional flour if necessary. Dip hands in confectioners sugar and roll dough into walnut-size balls. Roll each ball into a rope and shape into crescents on ungreased cookie sheets. Bake 12-15 minutes or until bottom edges just begin to brown. Remove cookies to rack; cool completely. Dust with confectioners sugar. *Makes 3-4 dozen.*

SNOW WHITE BUTTERCREAM ICING

4 Tablespoons Wilton Meringue
  Powder Mix
½ Teaspoon Wilton Almond Extract
½ Teaspoon Wilton Clear Vanilla Extract
¼ Teaspoon Wilton Butter Flavor

⅔ Cup Water
12 Cups Sifted Confectioners
  Sugar (approx. 3 lbs.)
1¼ Cups Solid Shortening
¾ Teaspoon Salt

Combine water and meringue powder; whip at high speed until peaks form. Add 4 cups sugar, one cup at a time, beating after each addition at low speed. Alternately, add shortening and remainder of sugar. Add salt and flavorings; beat at low speed until smooth. *Makes 7 cups.* Recipe may be doubled or cut in half. If cut in half, makes 2⅔ cups.

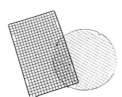

Sturdy cooling grids are a baking essential. Wilton Cooling Grids, made of chrome-plated steel, are tightly woven to prevent even the daintiest cookies from falling through.

SPECTACULAR SPRITZ!

*Delicate, buttery spritz cookies with just a hint of almond are traditional Christmas favorites.
Here spritz bar-shaped cookies are given a new twist when made with a tri-colored dough and a special
pressing technique. The confection coated spritz trees sparkle with ready-to-use
piping gel trim. Both are perfect with a mug of hot cocoa on a cold winter night.*

Wilton Products:

Spritz Cookie Press Set
Cookie Sheet
Cooling Grid
White Candy Melts®*
Red, Green Decorating
  Gel Tubes
Christmas Red, Leaf Green
  Icing Colors

1½ Cups Butter or Margarine,
  Softened
1 Cup Granulated Sugar
1 Egg
2 Tablespoons Milk
1 Teaspoon Wilton Clear
  Vanilla Extract
½ Teaspoon Wilton Almond
  Extract
4 Cups All-Purpose Flour
1 Teaspoon Baking Powder

*brand confectionery coating

Preheat oven to 400°F. Thoroughly cream butter and sugar. Add egg, milk, vanilla and almond extract; beat well. Stir together flour and baking powder; gradually add to creamed mixture, mixing to make a smooth dough. Do not chill.

For Candy Coated Trees: Place dough in cookie press fitted with tree-shaped disk; press cookies onto ungreased cookie sheet. Bake 6-8 minutes; remove cookies from sheet. Cool on rack. Melt candy according to package directions; dip to coat cookies. Decorate with gel while coating is still slightly soft; let set. *Makes 6 dozen cookies.*

For "Ribbon Candy" Cookies: Divide dough equally into thirds. Color one third green and one third red; leave one third white. Roll each color dough into logs, approximately ½ in. x 6 in. Place green, white and red doughs side by side and press together. Fit barrel of cookie press onto handle. Carefully place dough in cookie press, making sure colors are crosswise to handle. Fit cookie press with bar disk, positioning bar opening crosswise so that all three colors are visible. Press dough onto ungreased cookie sheet in long strips, moving press up and down at each click in order to make curled ribbon effect. Make cuts in strips after every second curl with knife. Separate cookies about ¼ in. Bake 6-8 minutes; remove cookies from sheet. Cool on rack. *Makes 2-3 dozen cookies.*

*The Spritz Cookie Press Set features disks with 12 classic holiday shapes.
Its easy-squeeze trigger-action handle lets you press out dozens of spritz cookies in
no time at all—great for bulk gift-making.*

COLOR IT CHRISTMAS!

Wilton Products:

Cookie Sheet or Pan

Christmas Cookie Collection
  Cutter Set

Bell, 5-Pt. Star, Tree, Snowman,
  Rocking Horse Perimeter
  Cookie Cutters

Alphabet Set Cookie Cutters

Disposable Decorating Bags

Tip 2

Christmas Red, Kelly Green,
  Brown, Golden Yellow Icing
  Colors

Roll-Out Cookie Dough
  Recipe, (p. 40)

Prepare cookie dough. Tint portions of dough separately in desired colors.
For Outlined Cookies: Cut cookies out of plain dough. Thin down desired
shade of tinted dough with 1 teaspoon water at a time until it will pass
through decorating tip. Place dough in bag fitted with tip 2. Outline and pipe
in desired designs. Bake.
For Alphabet Cookies: Roll out four 12 in. logs of tinted dough about ¼ in.
wide. Place all rolls close together horizontally. Roll out dough with rolling
pin to blend together. Cut out and bake.
For Marbleized Cookies: Place flattened, 1½ in. diameter tinted and plain
dough balls side-by-side on cookie sheet. Place smaller balls of contrasting
colors on top of large pieces of dough. Roll out mixture of colors. Cut out and
bake. *Each cookie serves 1. One recipe of dough makes 20-24 medium-size cookies.*

*Count on Wilton Icing Colors to produce exactly the shade you
want — whether tinting cookie dough or icings. Our concentrated, fast-mixing color is
available in over 30 beautiful shades and convenient multi-color kits.*

Bake in color
and wake up your
cookie tray!

SANTA PANORAMA

Wilton Products:

Christmas Cookie Tree Kit
Golden Yellow, Kelly Green
   Icing Colors
Candy Colors Set
Candy Melts*, White
   (1 bag needed)
Santa Claus Icing Decorations
Rainbow Nonpareils Sprinkle
   Decorations
6 in. Cake Boards
Fanci-foil Wrap
6 in. Doilies

Roll-Out Cookie Dough,
   Chocolate Roll-Out
   Cookie Dough Recipes
   (see below)
Cellophane, Ribbon

*brand confectionery coating

Using tinted plain and chocolate doughs, cut out cookies with 4th largest cutter. Cut out star opening with 6th largest cutter. Bake and remove from oven. While cookies are stil warm, cut two cookies in half and leave one cookie whole for each 3-D star. Let cool. Using cut decorator bag filled with melted candy, outline outside edge and inside bottom of each star. Immediately sprinkle with nonpareils. (For faster drying, place unassembled cookies in freezer for a few seconds.) Attach star halves to whole star using melted candy; hold a few minutes to secure.

Mold inner candy stars: Place 2nd smallest cutter on a board covered with waxed paper. Tint Candy Melts with candy color. Fill cutter with melted candy. To set, place in freezer for several seconds; release cutter from candy. Attach icing decoration with melted candy; attach candy star at center of cookie star with melted candy. Place doily and star on foil-covered board, wrap in cellophane, tie with ribbon bow. One batch makes 10-12 assembled stars.

ROLL-OUT COOKIES

1 Cup Butter or Margarine,
   Softened
1 Cup Sugar
1 Large Egg
1 Teaspoon Vanilla
2 Teaspoons Baking Powder
3 Cups Flour

Preheat oven to 400°F. In a large bowl, cream butter and sugar with an electric mixer. Beat in egg and vanilla. Add baking powder and flour, one cup at a time, mixing after each addition. The dough will be very stiff; blend last flour in by hand. Do not chill dough. (*For chocolate cookies*: Stir in 3 ounces melted, unsweetened chocolate.) Divide dough into 2 balls. On a floured surface, roll each ball into a circle approximately 12 in. in diameter and ⅛ in. thick. Dip cutters in flour before each use. Bake cookies on an ungreased cookie sheet on top rack of oven for 6-7 minutes, or until cookies are lightly browned.

Three cookies create an extraordinary three-dimensional treat!
Our 3-D Cookie Stars, in chocolate or colorful vanilla dough, are easy
to assemble—just attach four star halves to one whole cookie. Use the graduated
cutters in our Cookie Tree Kit to cut cookies and openings. Add a candy Santa
and you've made something magical.

WHITE CHOCOLATE CHIP AND MACADAMIA NUT BARS

*Gourmet ingredients, a festive-shaped pan and vivid, Christmas-colored garnishes
turn ordinary bar cookies into extraordinary holiday treats. For after school snacking,
omit garnishes and switch to semi-sweet chocolate chips and pecans or walnuts.
This recipe also works wonderfully in the Wilton 9 x 13-inch sheet pan.*

Wilton Products:
Treeliteful Pan
Kelly Green Icing Color
Candy Melts®*, Red

1 Cup Butter or Margarine,
    Softened
1 Cup Granulated Sugar
2 Eggs
1½ Teaspoons Vanilla
2 ¾ Cups All-Purpose Flour
½ Teaspoon Baking Soda
½ Teaspoon Salt
½ Cup White Chocolate Chips
½ Cup Macadamia Nuts,
    Chopped
15-20 Whole Macadamia Nuts
Buttercream Icing Recipe (p.91)
Milk
1 Cup Flaked Coconut,
    Tinted Green

*brand confectionery coating

Preheat oven to 325°F. Spray pan with non-stick vegetable pan spray. In large bowl, cream butter and sugar. Add eggs, one at a time, beating well after each addition. Add vanilla and mix well. Combine flour, baking soda and salt. Stir into butter mixture. Stir in white chocolate chips and chopped macadamia nuts. Spread dough in prepared pan. Bake 35-40 minutes or until golden brown and cookies spring back when touched lightly with finger. Cool 5 minutes in pan on rack. Remove from pan and cool thoroughly.

Meanwhile, melt candy according to package directions. Dip whole nuts; let set. Thin icing with small amount of milk; spread over cookie. Sprinkle with coconut; garnish with coated nuts. Cut into bars to serve. Makes 10-12 servings.

*The Treeliteful Pan makes beautiful gelatin molds easy. Simply mix
strawberry or lime gelatin, pour in pan, and add grapes, cherries or other fruit
ornaments. Unmold and trim your tree with whipped topping.*

Package these special bar cookies as a gift for someone near and dear!

Season's Greetings Cookie Cards

Wilton Products:

Christmas Treats Cookie
Cutter Set
Tree Perimeter Cookie Cutter
Make Any Message
Letterpress Set
Christmas Red, Kelly Green,
Brown, Golden Yellow
Icing Colors
Decorating Tips 2, 5, 16
8 in. Cake Circle
Decorator Brush Set
Edible Glitter
Alphabet/Numerals Icing
Decorations
Rainbow Nonpareils and
Cinnamon Sprinkle
Decorations
Candy Melts®*—Christmas
Mix, Yellow, Lt. Cocoa,
Pink, White
Christmas Lollipop
Candy Mold
Meringue Powder

Royal Icing, p. 78
Roll-Out Cookie Dough
    Recipe, p. 40
Candy: Jelly Discs, Spearmint
    Leaves, Fruit Sheets

*brand confectionery coating

Santa's Card: Cut tree and 6 ½ x 4 ½ in. rectangle card out of cookie dough; bake and cool. Spatula ice top of card to within ½ in. of edge. Using tip 2, pipe icing on sides, immediately add Rainbow Nonpareils Sprinkle Decorations. Attach tree cookie with dots of icing and cover with tip 16 pull-out stars. Add tip 2 zigzag garland and tip 2 dots. Cut jelly disc into star shape, attach to tree top with icing and outline using tip 2. Add Sprinkle Decorations to tree. Mold candy, following directions on Candy Melts package. Refrigerate to set. Attach candy to card with dots of icing. Add tip 2 message.

Holiday House Card: Cut 9 ½ x 6 ½ rectangle card out of cookie dough; imprint house cutter and message into dough. Thin icing colors with water and paint house. In a small bowl, combine small amounts of tinted cookie dough with 1 teaspoon water at a time until thin enough to pass through decorating tip. Pipe tip 2 message, top bead trim and house accents. Pipe snow on house and spatula smooth. Pipe tip 5 bead border around card. Add edible glitter. Bake at 350°F for 10-12 minutes.

Wreath Card: Cut cookie from dough using 8 in. cake circle as pattern. Bake and cool. Cut spearmint leaves into thirds; setting in 3 overlapping rows, attach leaves to cookie using green royal icing. Attach Cinnamon Sprinkle Decorations and Alphabet Icing Decorations with royal icing. Cut fruit sheets into strips—4 in. for bows, 2 in. for streamers and loop. Fold into bow shapes and attach with dots of icing.

Don't put the cookie cutters away! Wilton Cookie Cutters can be used for so many other wonderful holiday projects. Bread dough ornaments, sandwiches for the party, place cards, butter molds and much more all take on the favorite shapes of the season.

St. Nick Cookie Pops

Everyone will get a kick out of cookies on a stick.
They're easy to bake — just press the dough into Wilton Cookie
Treat Pans; decorating is quick, too.

Wilton Products:
Tree Cookie Treat Pan
Round Cookie Treat Pan
Tips 2, 3, 5, 12, 13, 15, 16, 352
Kelly Green, Red-Red, Black,
Copper (light skin tone)
Icing Colors
Cookie Treat Sticks
Cinnamon Sprinkle Decorations

Buttercream Icing, p. 91
Cookie On A Stick Recipe
(on Cookie Treat Pan package)
Striped Gum
Black Shoestring Licorice
Red Ribbon

Bake cookies according to recipe. Let cool.

To decorate tree and wreath: Pipe tip 352 pull-out leaves. Add cinnamon dots and red ribbon bow. To decorate Santa: Pipe in tip 12 face. Add tip 15 pull-out hair, beard and moustache. Pipe tip 3 dot eyes and nose. Pipe in tip 3 mouth (smooth with finger dipped in cornstarch). Add tip 13 pull-out star eyebrows. Cover hat with tip 16 stars, add tip 16 zigzag brim and rosette pom-pom. Add red ribbon bow. To decorate tumbling skier: Ice round cookie fluffy with spatula. Pipe tip 12 ball head (smooth with finger dipped in cornstarch). Pipe tip 2 dot eyes, nose and ears. Pipe tip 2 zigzag line for mouth. Outline and pipe in tip 5 collar. Add tip 2 dots to points of collar. Pipe in tip 5 hat, add tip 15 zigzag brim and rosette pom-pom. Add black licorice pieces for ski poles, pipe tip 5 mittens over licorice. Add tip 2 line across bottom end of pole. Cut gum to points for ski and slightly curl tips. Attach to back of cookie with icing. *Each serves 1.*

Wrap up party goodies or "thank you" treats in cheerful Wilton Treat Bags.
There's a fun design for just about any celebration or theme — holidays,
graduations, sports parties, Over The Hill parties and more.

Here's a fun surprise to unwrap—I even tie these pops onto my gifts!

CHAPTER 3

GINGERBREAD

Don't miss out on one of the season's greatest pleasures:

baking and decorating delightful gingerbread gifts

and centerpieces. You'll find something for

everyone—from ready-to-assemble trees to a

magnificent mansion, from family photo frames

to a woven basket filled with your favorite muffins.

We've even included an Art of Gingerbread

section, with tips and recipes to

make your decorating easy.

Wilton Ready-To-Use Gingerbread Kits make a great holiday tradition more convenient. Everything you need is here: baked gingerbread sections, candy decorations, decorating bags and tip, meringue powder and instructions for five fun designs.

Wilton Products:

Ready-To-Use Gingerbread Tree Kit

Ready-To-Use Gingerbread House Kit

Decorating Comb

*Kelly Green, Golden Yellow, Brown
   Icing Colors*

Santa Claus Icing Decorations

*Petite Wreath & Snowman Icing
   Decorations (4 pks. needed)*

Royal Icing Recipe*, p. 78

Green Spice Drops (for trees around house;
   purchase approximately 100)*

Fruit Sheet Candy, Mini Dot Candy, Mini Jaw
   Breakers Candy, Assorted Color Gum Drops

*Note: Meringue Powder (for royal icing)
   included in kit. Candies listed above are
   needed in addition to those included in kit.

TRIM THE TREE

Assemble tree following kit instructions. Ice smooth, then make lines with fork to form separations on tree and trunk. Using tip 16, pipe zigzag garland on tree and edge of tree sections; add jaw breakers. Pipe tip 16 pull-out stars to resemble snow. Pipe tip 16 strings on tree trunk. Cut gum drops in half; attach gum drops and icing decorations to tree with dots of icing. Ice gingerbread star smooth; attach jaw breakers and icing decorations. Attach star to tree top with icing.

SANTA'S RETREAT

Assemble house following kit instructions. Ice roof in a swag motion using large teeth edge of Decorating Comb. Using a toothpick, mark 2 in. square windows and 1½ x 3¼ in. door. Cut fruit sheet into curtain shapes and attach with icing. Using a cut bag, outline door and windows; add mini dot candies. Edge roof with zigzag motion, cut spice drops in half and attach along roof edge. Divide spice ring in half for wreath and attach to front of house; cut a bow from fruit sheet and attach to wreath with icing. Attach Santa Claus Icing Decorations to front door and back of house with icing. Plant hedges and trees around house using green spice drops and icing; pipe icing to create snow effect.

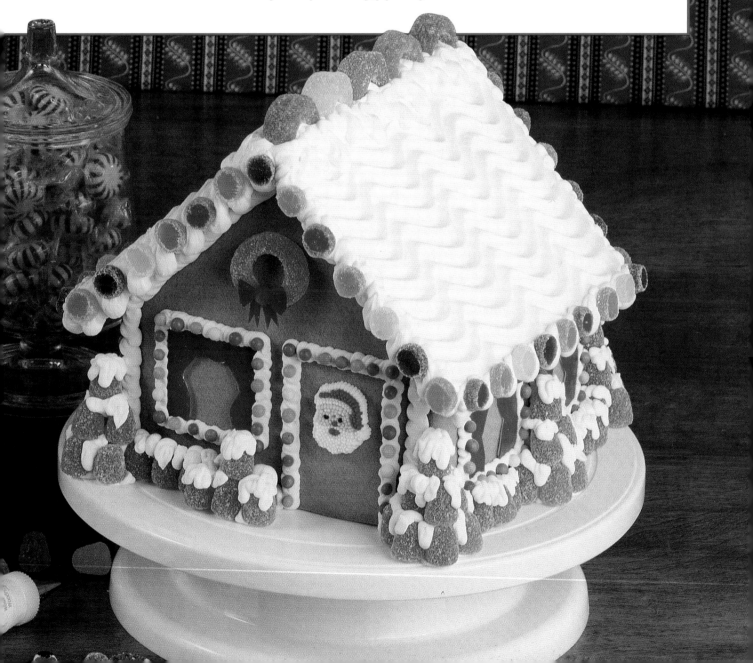

Santa's Snapshots

*Two wonderful ways to hold onto holiday memories. And you can
keep them fresh for years by coating the frames after assembling with a layer of shellac
or acrylic spray. (Of course, frames and candy are not to be eaten.)*

HOME FOR THE HOLIDAYS

Wilton Products:
Gingerbread House Kit
Tip 4

Royal Icing, p. 78
Gingerbread Recipe, p. 59
Candy Sticks, Round Candy
  Discs, Mini Candy Balls,
  Spearmint Leaves,
Gold-Tone Easel
  (available at craft stores)

Make gingerbread recipe. Cut 2 house fronts; on one front cut out door and window. Use church steeple base pattern for big window. Cut out 1 eave. Leave second house front solid. Bake and let cool.

Attach pictures to solid house front piece with royal icing. Attach cut out house front over pictures with royal icing. Attach eaves with royal icing. Pipe tip 4 beads around photos. Attach candies with dots of royal icing. Add tip 4 pull-out snow on window sills. Pipe additional pull-out snow on roof with tip 4.

Position on easel.

SNOWFLAKE STAR

Wilton Products:
Christmas Cookie Collection Set
Mini Perimeter Star
  Cookie Cutter
Tips 2, 3, 7, 17
Black, Christmas Red,
  Kelly Green, Brown, Golden
  Yellow Icing Colors

Royal Icing
Gingerbread Recipe, p. 59
Gold-Tone Easel
  (available at craft stores)
5" x 7" Picture Frame Pattern
  (on this page - use pattern
  at 100%)

Make gingerbread recipe and cut 2 frame sides (1 with window and 1 solid). From Christmas Cookie Collection Set, cut out 1 each: star, snowman, bear and 2 Mini Perimeter Stars. Bake and let cool.

Attach picture to back of frame with royal icing. Overlay cut-out portion of frame on picture and attach with royal icing. Pour icing on stars, let dry. Ice bear and snowman cookies with spatula. Pipe tip 2 dot and string facial features on cookies. Pipe tip 2 bead border on stars. Pipe in tip 7 hats and dot pompoms. Add tip 2 pull-out holly leaves and dot berry on snowman. Fill in tip 3 scarf and candy cane (flatten and smooth with finger dipped in cornstarch). Spatula ice snow drift at base of frame. Pipe tip 3 beads around frame, add tip 17 shells around outside beads. Pipe tip 2 dot and string snowflakes. Attach cookies to frame with royal icing.

*The Wilton Gingerbread House Kit can be the building block to many exciting
holiday crafts—including fun-to-decorate centerpieces for all levels of skill. Add the gingerbread shapes you want
to go with your house, using our great selection of cookie cutters and the gingerbread recipe on page 59.*

These great gifts let faraway family see how the kids have grown!

I love the candles and the carolers—they make this impressive house feel warm inside and out!

Instructions to make this fabulous house on following page.

COUNTRY ESTATE

Our grand mansion, shown on page 54, is based on simple gingerbread construction techniques. The patterns you will need are labeled alphabetically in the Wilton Gingerbread House Kit—just follow cutting directions and assembly instructions below and in "The Art of Gingerbread" section on page 58. You can do it!

Wilton Products:
Gingerbread House Kit
Decorating Tips 1, 2, 3, 5,
* 7, 13, 15, 32*
Royal Blue, Aster Mauve,
* Cornflower Blue, Buttercup*
* Yellow, Black, Juniper Green,*
* Kelly Green, Christmas Red*
* Icing Colors*
Meringue Powder
Tree Formers Set
Fanci-Foil Wrap

Grandma's Gingerbread Recipe
  2 Batches Needed, (lighter dough
  variation), p. 59
Royal Icing Recipe, p. 78

Regular and mini marshmallows,
  confectioners sugar, 16 x 22 in.
  pressed board or sturdy
  double thick cardboard, cotton
  puffs, waxed paper, ceramic
  people figurines

Note: Royal Blue and a little Black produces the blue/grey color for trim. Juniper Green with a little Kelly Green and a little Royal Blue produces the green for trees and shrubs.

Using Royal Icing, tip 32 and Tree Formers Set, make 6 trees with pull-out star branches. Cover approximately 25 mini and 15 regular marshmallows with tip 15 stars for shrubs. Set all aside.

Make 2 batches of Grandma's Gingerbread, following the variation for lighter dough. Tint one batch of dough with Cornflower Blue and a little Royal Blue; tint the other batch of dough Aster Mauve. Note that the tinted dough bakes to a much lighter shade. We suggest tinting and baking small amounts of dough as a test until desired colors are achieved.

Using patterns in kit (marked alphabetically), cut the following basic pieces: 2 complete houses (A, B, D) plus 1 complete chimney (F, G); 3 scalloped eaves (J); 1 complete dormer (L, K). Cut the following pieces making these modifications: 2 dormer side pieces (K), trim scallops off at dotted line; 4 house door pieces (H), to be used for steps/walkway; approximately 36 scalloped shingle strips (C), cut only scalloped edge 1 in. high and length of roof; 2 dormer fronts (L) to be used for bay window roof, trim ¾ in. off bottom edge and cut edge into scallops, cut one dormer front in half. Also cut two 4 in. high x 2 in. wide and one 4 in. high x 3½ in. wide panels for bay window. Bake and cool pieces following kit instructions.

Assemble house using royal icing and tip 7. The main house section has the dormer and is on the right; the side house has the bay window and is on the left. Assemble sides of 2 houses on base, offset main house 1¾ in. back. When sides are dry, add roofs. For inside roof of side house, trim scalloped edge approximately 1½ in. so roof meets flush with adjoining main house. Roof on main house is offset to the right (no trimming is necessary). Add two trimmed dormer side pieces to join the roofs. Attach dormer to main house; attach bay window to side house. Attach shingle strips and eaves, trimming when necessary to fit. Add chimney to side house.

Following pattern pieces Q for windows and H for doors, ice windows, doors and bay windows smooth. Outline bay window using tip 5; trim house seams and edges with tip 3 beads. Using tip 3, add outlines and pipe candles; add tip 1 greens, garland and wreaths, add tip 2 flames, bows and berries. Pipe tip 13 pull out stars for Christmas tree; add tip 2 dot ornaments. Trim door pieces to sizes desired for steps (top step is approximately 2 in.); ice smooth and position at doorways.

Spatula ice fluffy snow around house. Position trees and shrubs. Thin icing with a little light corn syrup and add to roof in drifts. Dust house and trees with confectioners sugar. Position cotton puff in chimney and add ceramic figures around house.

For a gingerbread house that looks great and lasts for months, your Royal Icing must be the perfect consistency. Wilton Meringue Powder helps you create Royal Icing that dries candy hard. And don't forget, Wilton Meringue Powder is a great egg substitute in your favorite meringue-based recipes.

Front View

Rear View

The Art of Gingerbread

Hints and Advice for Easy Baking and Construction

For many of us, our first exposure to gingerbread came in the tale of Hansel and Gretel. While the wicked witch may have scared us, her gingerbread cottage, bedecked with bright candies and sweets, fascinated us. But we didn't really know about gingerbread until we smelled its sweet, spicy aroma for ourselves. Now we realize that, in building that first family gingerbread house, we were also building a wonderful holiday tradition...a tradition to pass on through the years.

With Christmas on the horizon, it's time to choose a gingerbread project to inspire you. Using imagination, icing and candies, a basic gingerbread house can become a mountain chalet, a woodland cottage or a Victorian mansion. Or, use gingerbread to construct fabulous gifts and decorations: a charming sleigh centerpiece, a woven basket, homemade photo frames and tree ornaments. Successful gingerbread artistry requires following some common sense steps, which are listed on these pages. But the most important tip we can give for working with gingerbread: have fun!

Getting Started
- Before starting a gingerbread project, carefully read through the recipe and procedures for assembly.
- Assemble all recipe ingredients, baking equipment, decorating supplies and project decorations.
- Prepare any necessary patterns. Patterns in this book are full size. Transfer drawings to waxed paper or parchment and cut out.

Dough Dos and Don'ts
- Don't choose humid days for making gingerbread projects. Gingerbread is like a sponge—even though your gingerbread may be dry, it will soften and fall if placed in a humid room. Baked gingerbread pieces need to be dry and firm, especially for larger projects. If you live in an area which is always humid, back baked gingerbread pieces with cake board.
- Do measure all ingredients accurately when preparing dough.
- Do use light (mild flavor) or dark (robust flavor) molasses depending on recipe directions or desired color and flavor of finished project.
- Don't refrigerate dough. However, if you plan to work on your project at a later time, dough may be covered and refrigerated for up to one week. Refrigerated dough will need to stand at room temperature several hours before it can be rolled. Or bring dough to room temperature by warming in microwave at 10% power for 1 minute or more, depending on amount of dough.

- Do roll dough directly on cookie sheets unless directed otherwise. This eliminates the need to transfer cut pieces, a process that can distort shapes and is nearly impossible to do with larger pieces.
- Do use a Wilton Cookie Sheet with only one side or the back of a Wilton Cookie Pan for ease in rolling. Place a dampened towel under your cookie sheet to keep it steady while rolling dough.
- Don't guess how thick your dough is rolled; use a ruler to measure.
- Do keep any dough not being used tightly wrapped in plastic to prevent it from drying out.

Preparing the Pieces
- To prepare pieces, place patterns over rolled dough and use a sharp knife or pizza cutter to cut out shapes. Be careful when removing excess dough around gingerbread pieces. Smaller projects may call for Wilton Cookie Cutters.
- For even baking and to avoid burning, bake only pieces similar in size at the same time. Baking only one cookie sheet at a time also helps to ensure even baking.
- Once baked, loosen gingerbread pieces with a spatula to prevent sticking. While still warm, place patterns over baked pieces and trim uneven edges with a sharp knife. Let stand on cookie sheet 10 minutes or as recipe directs.
- If your gingerbread pieces become warped or lose their shape, lay on cookie sheet, reheat at 350°F for 3-5 minutes and flatten back into shape. Cool completely before using.
- Cool pieces on sturdy cooling racks. Pieces must remain flat while cooling or shapes may become distorted. Gingerbread for large projects should be allowed to dry at least 48 hours in order to firm and harden.

Rules for Royal Icing
Royal Icing, made with Wilton Meringue Powder Mix, confectioners sugar and water, is the "glue" for gingerbread construction. It dries hard and holds for weeks (sometimes even months or years under ideal storage conditions).

Following are some tips for working with Royal Icing:

- Mixing bowls, beaters and utensils must be free of any grease as grease causes Royal Icing to break down. For this same reason you may want to use parchment or disposable decorating bags when piping with Royal Icing.
- Heavy-duty mixers work best for preparing this stiff icing, especially if you are doubling the recipe. When using a portable mixer make only one batch at a time.

- Use Wilton Icing Colors to color icing. Royal icing requires more color than buttercream icing to achieve the same shade and Wilton Colors won't thin your icing.
- When coloring icing, mix enough of desired color for entire project as it will be difficult later to duplicate an exact shade.
- Royal Icing dries very quickly. Keep any portions you aren't working with covered with a dampened cloth or paper towel.
- This icing can be stored for up to two weeks if kept in a tightly covered container at room temperature. Just rewhip before using.

Advice for Assembly
- Use a sturdy base for gingerbread projects. Cake boards, serving trays, cookie sheets and cutting boards are all possibilities. Just be sure the base is able to support the weight of the project. Large houses may weigh up to several pounds.
- Choose a base large enough to allow space for any "landscaping" or other decorations. Cover base with foil, if desired.
- Gingerbread pieces are joined together with Royal Icing. It's easiest to use a decorating bag and round tip to pipe the icing onto gingerbread pieces.
- Lay out all pieces of a project before "gluing" to confirm fit and position on your base, but construct project one piece at a time.
- Royal Icing dries quickly, so pipe it onto pieces just before joining them.
- Hold each piece of a project in place for a few minutes so icing sets before moving on to the next piece. An extra pair of hands is often helpful. Heavy cans or jars can be used to support pieces until icing dries completely.
- When constructing houses, let walls of structures set until firm before adding roof pieces. An extra bead of icing can be piped inside along joints for added security. And don't worry about icing that squeezes through seams. It will usually be covered with decorations later.
- Roof pieces should be added carefully and one at a time. Any spaces between the underneath side of the roof and the walls can be filled in with icing to adequately secure.

Decorative Details

Gingerbread projects can be whimsical and charming or artful and sophisticated. Icing colors and piped details along with candies in every color, size and shape lead to endless decorating schemes for any project. In addition to candies you may want to use some of the following food items for decorating: colored sugar crystals, nonpareils, nuts, raisins, chocolate chips, coconut, marshmallows, marzipan, pretzels, cereals, crackers, cookies, chewy fruit rolls and sticks of gum. You'll no doubt think of others as you gain more experience in the art of gingerbread.

GRANDMA'S GINGERBREAD RECIPE

5 to 5 ½ Cups All Purpose Flour	1 Teaspoon Cloves
1 Teaspoon Baking Soda	1 Cup Shortening
1 Teaspoon Salt	1 Cup Sugar
2 Teaspoons Ginger	1¼ Cups Unsulphured Molasses
2 Teaspoons Cinnamon	2 Eggs, Beaten
1 Teaspoon Nutmeg	

Preheat oven to 375°F. Thoroughly mix flour, soda, salt and spices. Melt shortening in large saucepan. Cool slightly. Add sugar, molasses and eggs; mix well. Add four cups dry ingredients and mix well. Turn mixture onto lightly floured surface.

Knead in remaining dry ingredients by hand. Add a little more flour, if necessary, to make a firm dough. Roll out on a lightly floured surface to ¼ in. thickness for cut-out cookies. Bake on ungreased cookie sheet: Small and medium-sized cookies for 6-10 minutes, large cookies for 10-15 minutes. One recipe of this gingerbread dough will yield 40 average size cookies.

Note: If you're not going to use your gingerbread dough right away, wrap it in plastic and refrigerate. Refrigerated dough will keep for a week, but be sure to remove it 3 hours prior to rolling so it softens and is workable.

Lighter Dough Variation

Produces a dough lighter in color that is easier to tint using icing color.

Follow the basic recipe, making these adjustments:
    omit 1¼ Cups Molasses and
    1 Cup Granulated Sugar,
    replace with 1¼ Cups
    Light Corn Syrup and 1 Cup
    Packed Light Brown Sugar

Knead in more flour, if necessary.

There's nothing merrier than a sleigh that's all decked out!

SLEIGH RIDE!

Company's coming, so Santa's sleigh is packed with fanciful Christmas cookies for everyone to enjoy. Made of gingerbread, this novelty centerpiece could deliver after-dinner sweets as well. Brightly colored detailing on Santa's sleigh and cookies are made with thinned tinted cookie dough, not icing.

LARGE BATCH ROLL-OUT COOKIES

1¼ Cups Butter
2 Cups Sugar
2 Eggs
5 Cups Flour
2 Teaspoons Baking Powder
1 Teaspoon Salt
½ Cup Milk
1 Teaspoon Wilton No-Color Almond Extract

Cream butter and sugar together, then add eggs and beat until fluffy. Sift dry ingredients together and add alternately to creamed mixture with milk. If mixture is too sticky, add a little more flour so that it is easy to handle.

Roll dough ⅛ in. thick and cut. Dip cutters in flour before each use. Bake cookies in 375°F oven for 8 minutes, or until edges are lightly browned.

Wilton Products:
Decorating Tips 2*, 3*, 6
Brown, Kelly Green, Christmas Red,
  Golden Yellow Icing Colors
15-Pc. Pattern Press Set
Gingerbread Family Cookie Cutter Set
Christmas Cookie Collection Set
Meringue Powder
Rainbow Nonpareils, Red Crystal and
  Green Crystal Sprinkle Decorations

Royal Icing Recipe, p. 78
Grandma's Gingerbread Recipe, p. 57
Large Batch Roll-Out Cookie Recipe
  (at left)
Sleigh Side Pattern (this page)
Ruler

*Decorating this project will go more quickly if you have two of tip 3 and three of tip 2.

Sleigh: Using sleigh pattern and gingerbread cut two sleigh sides (reverse pattern for second cut); one 5 x 4 in. back; one 6 x 4 in. bottom; one 3 x 4 in. front; two 1½ x 4 in. supports. Imprint dough with small "c" scrolls from Pattern Press Set. In a small bowl, combine small amounts of tinted gingerbread with 1 teaspoon water at a time until thin enough to pass through decorating tip 3; outline scroll imprints, add dot and string designs. Bake and cool. Using royal icing and tip 6, attach back, bottom, front and two supports to one sleigh side; hold each piece in place a few minutes until set; add second sleigh side. Let set completely before filling with cookies.

Cookie People and Seasonal Shapes: Cut an assortment of cookies using Large Batch Roll-Out Cookie Recipe and cutters. Decorate using tip 2 and thinned tinted cookie dough as above; add Sprinkle Decorations. Bake and cool.

Note: Use sleigh pattern on this page at 100%.

When you're making dozens of Christmas cookies, you want variety. Wilton cutter sets provide a great selection of shapes everyone loves in one convenient package. Fill your sleigh with favorites from the 4-Piece Gingerbread Family Cutter Set and the 10-Piece Christmas Cookie Collection Set.

Woven Gingerbread

WINTERFEST BASKET

Wilton Products:
8 in. Square Pan
Muffin Caps® Pan
Baking Sheets
Cooling Grid
Decorating Tips 2, 6
Red-Red, Kelly Green, Brown
  Icing Colors
Meringue Powder
Cake Boards
Fanci-Foil Wrap

Grandma's Gingerbread
  Recipe, p. 59
Royal Icing Recipe, p. 78
Your Favorite Muffin Mix
Waxed Paper, Ruler

Preheat oven to 350°F. Roll-out gingerbread ⅛ in. thick on waxed paper for easy pick-up and release. *To Make Sides:* Cut gingerbread dough into strips 5 in. long x ½ in. wide and 10 in. long x ½ in. wide. (Each side requires 8 short and 3 long strips.) Carefully weave 4 sides directly on baking sheets. If dough strips break while weaving, piece together at overlapping sections. For each side, roll two gingerbread dough ropes each 8 in. long; carefully twist together and position on top edge of side, roll one 8 in. log and attach to bottom of side. (Each finished panel should be 8 in. long x 4 in. wide, including rope trim.) Bake 10-12 minutes or until lightly browned. Immediately loosen from pan, but do not remove until cool; transfer to grid to air dry.
To Make Corner Posts: Roll gingerbread dough ½ in. wide, cut into four 4 in. log lengths. Bake 8-10 minutes at 350°F or until lightly browned. Cool on grid.
To Make Base: Spray inside of square pan with non-stick vegetable pan spray. Roll out gingerbread dough on waxed paper and cut a 9 in. square. Lift waxed paper with dough and place, dough side down, in pan; remove waxed paper. Press dough into bottom of pan and ½ in. up sides. Trim excess dough around edges. Prick gingerbread with fork. Increase oven temperature to 375°F and bake for 12-15 minutes or until sides are lightly browned. Immediately remove from pan—support gingerbread with 8 in. square cake board to prevent cracking. Cool on grid.
To Assemble Basket: Position gingerbread base on foil covered board for added support. Using royal icing and tip 6, pipe a line of icing on base edge of one side. Attach side to base and hold in place a few minutes until set. When all four sides are in position, pipe a line of icing at corners and attach posts. Using tip 2, pipe string vines, pull-out leaves and dot berries. Let basket set 6 hours or overnight until completely dry and firm before filling. Using your favorite muffin recipe, make muffin caps and fill basket. Basket holds 2 dozen muffin caps.

POTPOURRI PIES

Wilton Products:
Muffin Caps® Pan
Christmas Red Icing Color
6-Pc. Nesting Round
  Cutter Set

Grandma's Gingerbread
  Recipe, p. 59
Nonstick Vegetable
  Pan Spray,
Whole Cloves, Potpourri

Preheat oven to 350°F. Roll gingerbread dough ⅛ in. thick.
To make lattice tops: Lattice tops are baked on the *bottom* (outside) of pan. Spray bottom of pan with non-stick vegetable pan spray. Cut gingerbread dough into strips, 6 in. long x ⅜ in. wide. Beginning at center, place strips on pan and weave gingerbread, using 10 strips for each top; trim excess and seal edges with additional strips of gingerbread to form crust edge. Tint a small amount of dough and roll into apple shape. Position on top. Bake 10-12 minutes or until edges are lightly browned. Insert clove into apple shape while still hot. Immediately loosen gingerbread lattice from pan but do not remove; let cool completely on pan.
To make bottoms: Bottoms are baked *inside* cavities of pan. Spray pan with non-stick vegetable pan spray. Use largest round cutter and small paring knife to cut dough; invert cutter and cut around outer rim. Press into pan, shaping dough up over top edge of cavity to form lip. Prick gingerbread with fork and bake 10-15 minutes until edges are lightly browned. Immediately loosen from pan but do not remove; let cool completely on pan.
Hint: Stagger placement in pan and bake only 3 lattice tops or pie bottoms at a time to prevent dough from spreading into adjacent pieces.
Note: Do not eat pies filled with potpourri. Pies can also be filled with small candies.

Our Muffin Caps Pan bakes only the prime of the muffin — the chewy, delicious top.
Because at Christmas, everyone should get exactly what they want! Serve Muffin Caps at
holiday brunches or add them to gift baskets for a different holiday treat.

This basket can be filled with all sorts of Christmas goodies!

Candy Land Chalet

If you've never tried building with gingerbread, here's a great starter home.
Decorating is a snap—with spatula snow drifts and colorful candies providing the interest.
And our Gingerbread House Kit has the assembly instructions you
need to make this project a pleasure.

Wilton Products:
Gingerbread House Kit
Decorating Tip 6
Brown, No-Taste Red
  Icing Colors
Small Angled Spatula
Meringue Powder
Three 16 in. Round
  Cake Circles
Fanci-Foil Wrap
Rainbow Nonpareils and
  Rainbow Peanut Bits
  Sprinkle Decorations

Royal Icing Recipe, p. 78
Grandma's Gingerbread
  Recipe, p. 59
Dark Bead Molasses
Candy: Candy Cane Sticks,
  Assorted Hard Candy,
  Fruit Sheets, Jelly Circles,
  Peppermint Disks

Prepare Grandma's Gingerbread Recipe using bead molasses; tint dough to a darker shade by adding Brown and No-Taste Red Icing Color. Cut out and bake basic gingerbread house design with chimney following instructions included in kit. Assemble house using royal icing and tip 6 on triple thick foil-wrapped cake circles.

Attach all candy using royal icing. Cut fruit sheets into 1½ x 1¼ in. squares and one 1¼ in. half circle for windows; attach. Outline windows using tip 6 and add Rainbow Peanut Bits Sprinkle Decorations. Position candy cane sticks on house and chimney corners and approximately 3½ in. high at front door. Add peppermint disks above door and attach Rainbow Peanut Bit for door knob. Cut jelly circles in half and attach to roof peaks; outline using tip 6 and add Rainbow Peanut Bits.

Using tip 6, pipe snow in drifts on chimney. Add 1-2 teaspoons of light corn syrup to remaining royal icing and spatula ice roof fluffy. Add Nonpareil Sprinkle Decorations and hard candy to roof. Ice cake board fluffy and sprinkle with Nonpareils; position Rainbow Peanut Bits for sidewalk. Position hard candy for fence.

Whether you're a novice carpenter or an experienced architect, you'll find the Wilton
Gingerbread House Kit helpful. You can make an easy house great for kids who want to help or create
a work of art, like the multilevel house shown on pages 54-55. All the basics are here—easy-to-follow
recipes and instructions, house patterns, decorating bags, tips and gingerbread people cutters.

I'll need a place like this to chill out in January!

Whenever friends
trim the tree,
they'll think of you!

TREE CLIMBERS

Homemade ornaments have a warm, handcrafted look families welcome year after year—and they couldn't be easier! The gingerbread is molded in Wilton Cookie Treat Pans and Lollipop Molds, baked and painted. Add a personal touch by inscribing your name, gift date and a message on back with a toothpick before baking.

Wilton Products:
Christmas Tree Cookie Treat Pan
Star Cookie Treat Pan
Christmas Lollipop Mold
Tip 3
Brown, Kelly Green, Christmas
   Red Icing Colors
Clear Vanilla
Meringue Powder
Decorator Brush Set

Royal Icing, p. 78
Grandma's Gingerbread Recipe
   (2 recipes; 1 with molasses and
   1 with dark molasses), p. 59
Thin Drinking Straw
Twine or Ribbon
Vegetable Cooking
   Spray

For Candy Mold Gingerbread: Make 1 recipe of Grandma's Gingerbread with regular molasses. Press a small amount of gingerbread dough into each cavity. Place mold in freezer for 15 to 20 minutes. Remove dough from mold, place on greased cookie sheet and bake at 350° for 15-20 minutes. When cool, color with a small amount of clear vanilla mixed with desired shade of paste color. Paint figures with paste color mixture and decorator brushes. Let dry.

For Star and Tree Gingerbread: Make 1 recipe of Grandma's Gingerbread with dark molasses. Spray pans with vegetable pan spray. Press dark gingerbread dough into pans. Thin down ½ cup light gingerbread dough with water to a piping consistency. Using thinned dough in bag fitted with tip 3, pipe line and dot designs. Bake for 10-12 mintues. Remove from oven and immediately make hole in gingerbread with straw. Attach candy mold gingerbread shapes to star and tree gingerbread with royal icing. Add ribbon or twine for hanging.

Crafting with gingerbread is great, but why not give kids a taste? Wilton Cookie Treat Pans make gingerbread pops easy—just press in the dough around a cookie pop stick, bake and enjoy.

CHAPTER 4

Cake
Decorating

*People will think these festive cakes
came straight from Santa's Workshop. Just
like toys, you can make them large or
small, simple or spectacular—from easy
cupcakes to an elaborate winter
wedding cake. Our ideas are just
what you need to get everyone
in the holiday spirit!*

CLAUS FAMILY CAKES

BRINGING JOYFUL TOYS!

Wilton Products:
Santa Checking List Pan
Decorating Tips 1D, 2, 3, 4, 9,
12, 16, 18, 352
No-Taste Red, Christmas Red*,
Copper (Light Skin Tone),
Kelly Green, Ivory, Lemon
Yellow, Brown Icing Colors
Cake Boards, Fanci-Foil Wrap
Angled Spatula

Buttercream Icing, p. 91
Assorted Holiday Candies

Ice top and sides of cake smooth. Outline Santa and toy bag with tip 4 strings. Cover face, hat, suit and gloves with tip 16 stars. Pipe tip 16 pull-out star beard and moustache. Pipe tip 1D bricks. Ice "fur" on hat, gloves and snow on chimney fluffy with angled spatula. Pipe tip 3 dot eyes, nose and mouth (smooth with finger dipped in cornstarch).

Figure pipe toys: Pipe tip 12 ball bodies for teddy bear and doll. Add tip 9 dot arms (flatten and smooth with finger dipped in cornstarch), tip 4 dot and string facial features. Pipe tip 2 bow tie on bear and tip 2 pull-out hair on doll.

Position assorted candies. Add tip 18 shell bottom border. Add tip 352 holly leaves and tip 2 dot berries. *Serves 12.*

THE HOLIDAY HOSTESS

Wilton Products:
Santa Checking List Pan
Decorating Tips 2, 4, 16, 18,
103, 104, 352
No-Taste Red, Christmas Red*,
Black, Copper (Light Skin
Tone), Kelly Green, Ivory
Icing Colors
Cake Board
Fanci-Foil Wrap

Buttercream Icing, p. 91

Ice top and sides of cake smooth. Outline Mrs. Claus and list with tip 4 strings. Cover face, hands, legs, dress, hat and sleeves with tip 16 stars. (Note: Build up height on arms by covering with two layers of tip 16 stars.) Pipe tip 16 pull-out star bangs and eyebrows. Pipe tip 103 ruffle on hat, collar and sleeve; pipe tip 104 ruffle on apron. Add tip 2 string glasses and dots on dress. Pipe tip 4 eyes, nose, earrings and mouth (smooth with finger dipped in cornstarch). Add tip 18 shell bottom border with tip 352 holly leaves and tip 2 dot berries. *Serves 12.*

*Note: Mix No-Taste Red with Christmas Red for Santa's suit and Mrs. Claus' hat and dress.

One pan makes two terrific cakes: you can see how versatile our Santa Checking List Pan is. The list area is also ideal for birthday greetings, congratulations and more. Look for more great ideas on the label.

Mrs. Claus and I make a great team— especially when you have a lot of guests to serve!

MRS. CLAUS' RECIPE for Holiday Cheer
1. ROOM FULL of FRIENDS
2. CHRISTMAS MUSIC
3. DECORATIONS
4. GIFTS
* MIX ALL TOGETHER AND ENJOY!

CHRISTMAS BIRTHDAY CAKE

Planning ahead makes this cake even more convenient at the busiest time of year. Baked cakes wrapped in heavy-duty foil stay fresh when frozen up to three months—just thaw completely before icing. Make your buttercream icing up to two weeks in advance...refrigerate in an airtight container, then rewhip before using.

Wilton Products:
6 in. Round Pan
9 x 13 in. Sheet Pan
Tips 1, 3, 5, 9, 103, 352
Kelly Green, Red-Red, Royal Blue, Golden Yellow Icing Colors
Cake Boards, Fanci-Foil Wrap
6-Pc. Script Pattern Press Message Set
Santa & Friends Candle Set (2 sets used)
Dowel Rods

Buttercream Icing, p. 91
Sugar Cubes

Pipe tip 1 strings, bows, and pull out dots on sugar cubes; set aside. Ice one-layer 6 in. round and 2-layer 9 x 13 in. sheet cakes smooth and prepare for stacked construction: Dowel rod bottom tier. Center a corrugated cake circle on top of bottom tier. Position top tier. Using pattern press, imprint and pipe tip 3 message.

Round Tier: Pipe tip 352 leaves for wreath. Pipe tip 3 dot holly berries, tip 1 string snowflakes and tip 5 bead bottom border. Add tip 103 bow and ribbon streamers.

9 x 13 in. Tier: Divide long sides into 4ths, short sides into 3rds. Pipe tip 5 zigzag garland 1½ in. deep between division marks. Add tip 3 pull-out dot icicles on garland. Add tip 1 string snowflakes. Pipe tip 5 double bead top and tip 9 bottom bead borders. Add tip 352 leaves, tip 3 dot holly berries. Position candles and sugar cubes. *Serves 32.*

Wilton novelty candles, like this Santa set, create instant holiday fun, even on a plain iced cake or cupcake. There's a great selection for every occasion.

HOLIDAY FACES

*There's always time to make creative cupcakes! Just a dash of color from
our holiday baking cups or sprinkles transforms these treats into something special.
On more relaxed days, make the delightful Mr. & Mrs. Claus and crew.*

Wilton Products:
Standard Muffin Pan
Tips 2, 2A, 2D, 4, 12, 15
*Kelly Green, Copper (Light
    Skin Tone), Christmas Red,
    Brown Icing Colors*
*Christmas Tree Mix
    Sprinkle Decorations*
*Santa and Elves Standard
    Baking Cups*

Buttercream Icing, p. 91
*Gumball or Hard Round
    Candy for Nose, Small
    Candy Canes for Antlers*

For Sprinkle Cupcakes: Pipe tip 2D circular motion on cupcake tops.
Sprinkle with Christmas Tree Mix.

For Santa Claus: Ice smooth. Pipe tip 4 dot eyes and nose (flatten and smooth
with finger dipped in corn starch). Pipe tip 1 dot eye highlights. Pipe-in tip 2
mouth (smooth with finger dipped in cornstarch). Add tip 15 pull-out star
moustache and swirl motion beard. Pipe-in tip 2A stocking cap with tip 15
rosette pom-pom. Add tip 15 zigzag hat brim.

For Mrs. Claus: Ice smooth. Pipe tip 4 dot eyes and nose (flatten and smooth
with finger dipped in corn starch). Pipe tip 1 dot eye highlights. Outline
mouth with tip 2 strings, pipe in with tip 2 and smooth with finger dipped in
cornstarch. Pipe in ears with tip 4, add tip 4 dot
earrings. Add tip 15 swirl motion hair, bun and pull-out eyebrows.

For Elves: Ice smooth. Pipe tip 4 dot eyes (flatten and smooth with finger
dipped in cornstarch) with tip 1 dot highlights. Add tip 4 pull-out noses. Pipe
tip 2A caps. Outline mouth with tip 2 strings, fill-in with tip 2 and smooth
with finger dipped in cornstarch. Pipe hair: tip 4 swirl motion curly hair, tip 4
string straight hair, tip 15 pull-out hair.

For Reindeer: Ice fluffy. Pipe tip 12 pull-out ears. Build up tip 2A mouth.
Add tip 4 dot eyes (flatten and smooth with finger dipped in cornstarch).
Position candy canes for antlers and candy ball for nose.

Each serves 1.

*Instant excitement—that's what Wilton Baking Cups add to plain cupcakes. You'll find
colorful designs to brighten any occasion, made of grease-resistant microwave-safe paper. For more
fun in a jiffy, shake Wilton Sprinkle Decorations on holiday treats.*

I guarantee my cupcakes will put a smile on your face!

This tree is
as fun to trim as
the real thing!

SPARKLING SPRUCE

With snow-laden boughs, twinkling lights and pearl garlands, here's a
special cake that reminds us of the season's quiet beauty.

Wilton Products:
Treeliteful Pan
Decorating Tips 1, 2B, 3,
  5, 18, 233
Christmas Red, Lemon Yellow,
  Kelly Green, Royal Blue,
  Black, Violet, Orange,
  Brown Icing Colors
4mm Pearl Beading
  (1 pk. needed)
Cake Boards
Fanci-Foil Wrap
Small Tapered Spatula
Edible Glitter

Confectioners Sugar
Tea Strainer

Note: To achieve the icing colors shown, follow these formulas: Royal Blue and Violet combined produces the blue shade; Kelly Green, Black and Royal Blue combined produces the green shade.

Bake and cool cake. Ice background areas and sides of cake smooth. Pipe tip 18 string tree trunk. Cover tree with tip 3 and 233 pull-out needles. Attach pearl beading in one strand, starting at top and draping at varied intervals. Overpipe some pearls with tip 233 pull-out needles. Add tip 3 bead lights.

Pipe tip 5 drifted snow around tree trunk and on boughs, shaping icing with small tapered spatula. Sprinkle snow with edible glitter. Pipe tip 2B band at bottom border. Edge band with tip 5 beads. Add tip 3 zigzag garland. Pipe tip 1 snowflakes and dots. Place confectioners sugar in tea strainer and dust top of tree. *Serves 12.*

The Treeliteful Pan is Wilton's best-selling Christmas pan — because it works so
many ways. Gelatin salads, ice cream molds, breads and cakes all turn out beautifully in this
quality aluminum pan. Trim your tree with colorful garnishes for festive appeal.

HALLELUJAH CHORUS

Wilton Products:
Mini Gingerbread Boy Pan
Tips 2, 3, 5, 13, 349
No-Taste Red, Kelly Green,
*   Brown, Black, Lemon Yellow*
*   Icing Colors*

Meringue Powder
Cake Board, Fanci-Foil Wrap

Buttercream Icing, p. 91
Royal Icing (below)
Thin, Uncooked Spaghetti

For candles: Break pieces of uncooked spaghetti into desired lengths. Fill decorating bag, fitted with tip 5, with royal icing. Insert a piece of spaghetti into open end of tip, then as you squeeze bag, pull spaghetti out of tip, coating with icing. Push end into craft block, pipe tip 2 flame and let dry.

With buttercream icing, ice face and hands smooth; to extend hands slightly, overpipe area with tip 3. Fill-in space between feet with spatula. Ice lower robe and center shirt areas smooth with spatula; use tip of spatula to create grooves for "gathered" look.

Pipe collar and cuff areas using tip 3 and heavy pressure. Add tip 2 stitching lines. Pipe tip 3 dot nose, eyes, ears and mouth (smooth with finger dipped in cornstarch). Pipe tip 13 pull-out star hair. Position candles on hands with a dot of royal icing. Add tip 349 pull-out leaves. *Each serves 1.*

ROYAL ICING

3 Level Tablespoons Meringue
   Powder
4 Cups Sifted Confectioners
   Sugar (Approx. 1 lb.)
6 Tablespoons Water*

Beat all ingredients at low speed for 7 to 10 minutes (10 to 12 minutes at high speed for portable mixer) until icing forms peaks. *Makes 3 cups.*

*When using large countertop mixer or for stiffer icing, use 1 tablespoon less water

If you're putting together a holiday gift basket, you need Wilton Mini Pans. The Mini Gingerbread Boy works beautifully with quick breads, brownies and cakes—just wrap in cellophane and tie a ribbon around the neck for a wonderful basket treat.

The perfect
after-caroling cakes—
everyone can take
a solo!

CACTUS CHRISTMAS

*It's a new frontier for Santa! Our Christmas cowpoke is easily piped right on the
caketop, using buttercream and Wilton decorating tips. For more hints about figure piping,
see the current edition of the Wilton Yearbook of Cake Decorating.*

Wilton Products:
Western Boot Pan
Christmas Cookie Collection Set
Tips 2, 3, 5, 6, 7, 9, 16, 47, 199
Teal, Kelly Green, No-Taste Red,
  Black, Ivory Icing Colors
Rainbow Nonpareils Sprinkle
  Decorations
Cake Board
Fanci-foil Wrap

Buttercream Icing, p.91
Wrapped Peppermint Sticks,
  Candy Canes (7 each)

Bake and cool Western Boot cake. Ice cake sides and background
areas smooth. Outline boot and stitching using tip 3. Pipe tip 47
smooth side band sole and overpipe four tip 47 bands for heel.
Spatula ice hill area and snow on top of boot. Lightly imprint cake
with Santa cutter to use as pattern for figure piping. Cover boot
with tip 16 stars.

Pipe Santa: Pipe tip 7 ball head. Pipe tip 7 straight line for pants.
Add tip 7 ball boots and bead hat (flatten and smooth with finger
dipped in cornstarch). Using heavy to light pressure, pipe tip 7 shirt.
Add tip 5 outline belt with tip 3 buckle. Pipe tip 6 vest. Pipe tip 2
circular motion beard, moustache and hat fringe; add tip 2 dot tassel.
Pipe in tip 2 mouth; add tip 2 dot eyes. Write tip 2 lasso message;
pipe tip 2 dot hands and fingers.

Pipe tip 199 elongated shell cacti on cake top and sides. Pipe tip 9
bead border. Position sprinkles, insert peppermint sticks and candy
canes.
Serves 12.

*The Western Boot Pan covers lots of party territory—you can decorate
it with piped stitching and fringe to fit male and female birthdays, line dancing
parties or holidays with a country flavor.*

Saddle up
the reindeer and
let's ride!

STARS
OF
THE SEASON

*Jolly Old Saint Nick makes some
quick costume changes for his leading role
in this season's four-star show.
We've provided directions for a traditional
Santa and three other characters...but don't
stop there. Mini Star cakes are a great
shape for decorating any Santa
theme you can think of!*

Wilton Products:
Mini Star Pan
Decorating Tips 1, 2, 3, 14, 16, 46, 101
Kelly Green, Red-Red, Golden Yellow,
   Copper (Light Skin Tone), Black, Royal
   Blue, Brown Icing Colors

Buttercream Icing Recipe, p. 91
Goldfish Cracker
Mini Pretzel Stick

Follow the basic decorating instructions for
all designs, then add specific details.

Basics: Ice cake sides smooth. Ice face,
hands, and feet areas smooth. Using tip 14,
add string moustache and reverse shell
beard. Add tip 1 dot eyes and nose and
string mouth. Pipe tip 16 star bottom border.

Santa Firefighter: Ice hat smooth; add tip 16 pull-out star pompom. Cover clothes with tip 16 stars; add tip 101 hatband and boot cuffs. Outline tip 3 zipper. Using tip 1, outline and pipe in badges, smooth with finger dipped in cornstarch; add lettering.

Santa Fisherman: Cover pants, vest and hat with tip 14 stars; add pull-out star pompom. Add tip 3 dot shirt. Pipe tip 14 zigzag hat brim. Position goldfish cracker and pretzel stick, connect with tip 2 string.

Original Santa: Cover suit and hat with tip 16 stars; add pull-out star pompom. Add tip 14 zigzag cuffs and hat band. Pipe tip 46 belt and tip 2 buckle.

Santa Clown: Cover suit and hat with tip 14 stars, add tip 1 dots. Pipe tip 14 zigzag cuffs and hat brim. Add tip 14 star buttons on suit and hat.

Let your stars shine all year long with the Mini Star Pan. Whether you serve a stellar cheese dip on New Year's Eve, a cool molded gelatin or salad on July 4th, or a delectable ice cream or brownie birthday dessert, our quality aluminum construction assures you of great results every time.

As you can see, I wear a lot of hats during the holidays!

Snowcapped Ceremony

This impressive winter wedding cake is actually easy to decorate. Its perfectly smooth surface is achieved with a blanket of Wilton Ready-To-Use Rolled Fondant covering each tier. Fondant handles beautifully and is easy to tint as icing..Treeformers help you create the snowy pines fast. And the sleigh is simply cut from rolled gum paste and piped with buttercream.

Wilton Products:

Ovencraft™ 8, 12 in.
Round Pans
Ovencraft™ 18 in. Half
*Round Pan**
Tips 1, 2, 3, 5, 18
Rose, Willow Green,
Royal Blue Icing Colors
Ready-To-Use Rolled
Fondant (8 pks. needed)
Tree Former Set
Wooden Dowel Rods
Cake Boards, Fanci-Foil Wrap
Meringue Powder
Gum Paste Mix
Love's Duet Couple
Small Sleigh Pattern, (this pg.)

Royal Icing, p. 78
Buttercream Icing, p. 91
Confectioners Sugar

(*Note: Fill 18 in. Half Round Pan 1/2 full with batter. Bake two sets of half-round cakes to measure 4 inches high)

To Make Trees: Make 18 trees in various sizes using tree formers. For a variety of sizes, stack 2 to 4 tree formers and cover with waxed paper. Tree sizes should range from 3 to 6½ inches. To achieve color for branches, mix a few drops of royal blue in willow green. Pipe tip 18 pull-out stars for branches, beginning each section with a straight extended row of bottom branches, and adding downward pointing rows above. Repeat for new sections 2 or 3 times to top of tree. Pipe snow, using tip 2 and thinned down Royal Icing. Sprinkle with sifted confectioners sugar. Set aside.

For Sleigh: Prepare gum paste using package directions. Using sleigh pattern, traced on waxed paper, cut 2 sleigh sides, 1 back 2¼ x 3 in. and 1 front 2¼ in. x 2 in. Roll out gum paste and cut out sleigh patterns. Let dry 1-2 days. Assemble sleigh with Royal Icing. Use tip 2 for outlines, bead designs, dots, scrolls and pull-out fur on edge. Set aside to dry.

For Bride and Groom: Remove veil from bride. Use Royal Icing and tip 3 to overpipe hood. Add tip 1 pull-out fur on hood, neckline and muff behind bouquet. Tint 1 package fondant rose. Position cakes on cake circles. Ice 2-layer cakes. Cover cakes with white fondant. (Refer to package directions for tips on using rolled fondant.) Roll out small amounts of pink fondant, cut to 12 inch lengths. Cut random wavy lines in pink fondant, ranging from 1 inch to 3 inches high. Brush back of fondant with water; attach to cakes.

Prepare cakes for offset stacked construction: Place bottom tier on foil-covered board. Dowel rod bottom and middle tier for support. Position 12 in. middle tier 1½ in. from left edge of 18 in. tier. 8 in. cake will be positioned 1½ in. from right edge of 12 in. tier. To keep stacked tiers stable, sharpen one end of a dowel rod and push through all tiers and cardboard circles to base of bottom tier.

On pink fondant, draw trees with tip 2 zigzag, then overpipe with pull-out motion. Pipe tip 2 pull-out around bottom edge of cakes for snow effect. Pipe tip 5 bead border around bottom of all cakes. At reception, position trees, sleigh, bride and groom. *Makes 183 servings.†*

† The top tier is often saved for the first anniversary. The number of servings does not include the top tier.

Classic tiered cakes begin with Ovencraft™ Pans from Wilton.
These professional-quality pans of extra-thick aluminum provide superior heat distribution
and no-warp durability, for the precise baking results you demand. You'll find a great
selection of essential shapes and sizes at your Wilton dealer.

PERSONAL ANGELS

Wilton Products:
Mini Snowman Pan
Tips 2, 3, 7, 102, 349
Red-Red, Kelly Green, Golden
  Yellow, Copper (light skin tone),
  Brown Icing Colors
Scrolls (1 pk. needed)

Buttercream Icing, p. 91

Note: For specific decorating techniques, see the current Wilton Yearbook of Cake Decorating.

Prepare favorite cake mix. Bake and cool Mini Snowman cakes. Ice cakes smooth; form pleats in dress with spatula. Pipe tip 7 string arms. Pipe tip 3 dot hands and cheeks (flatten and smooth with finger dipped in cornstarch). Pipe tip 3 "e" motion curls for hair. Add tip 2 dot eyes and nose, string mouth. Pipe tip 102 ruffles at collar, sleeves and hem of dress. Add tip 3 dots above hem. Pipe tip 349 leaves, tip 2 berries at top of head. For wings, attach scrolls with dots of icing.

On a snowy day, kids will love helping you decorate cakes made in the Mini Snowman Pan. Just bake cakes, ice smooth or cover with stars, then add fun trims like pretzel sticks, raisins, licorice strips or cut gumdrops. One mix makes up to 18 snowmen!

CHOCOLATE CHRISTMAS TREE

CHOCOLATE FUDGE ICING

⅔ Cup Butter or Margarine
1 1/3 Cup Cocoa
6 Cups Confectioners Sugar
⅔ Cup Milk
2 Teaspoons Vanilla

Melt butter in saucepan over medium heat. Add cocoa and heat just until mixture begins to boil, stirring constantly until smooth. Pour into mixer bowl. Cool. Alternately add confectioners sugar and milk, beating to spreading consistency. Blend in vanilla. Makes 4 cups.

Wilton Products:
Ovencraft™ 12 in. x 3 in. deep
  Round Pan
Tips 1s, 3, 6
9 in. Decorator Preferred
  Separator Plate
Hidden Pillars
Disposable Decorating Bags

Christmas Lollipop Mold
Cookie Tree Kit
Candy Melts®*, Light Cocoa
  7 Bags Needed

Chocolate Fudge Icing
  Recipe (at left)

*brand confectionery coating

Cover 9 in. separator plate with melted candy. Let set. Mold 16 candies following directions on Candy Melts package. Make candies ¼ in. thick. Refrigerate to set. Line a cookie sheet with waxed paper. Position entire set of cookie tree cutters on waxed paper. Fill cutters halfway with melted candy; refrigerate. Remove set candy from cutters and repeat process. (Two of each size star needed.) Drizzle melted candy on star points with tip 1s. Pipe tip 3 bead border around each star.

Ice 1-layer round cake with fudge icing; sides smooth and top fluffy. Position hidden pillars cut to height of cake; place 9 in. plate on top. Pipe tip 6 scallop border around plate. Pipe tip 6 bead top and bottom borders. Position stars, following kit assembly instructions. Attach candies to cake side with dot of icing. *Makes 33 servings.*

Gather the family around the cookie tree! The Christmas Cookie Tree Kit is a fun project everyone can make in 30 minutes. Just bake cookies, stack and decorate. Everything you need is here—cutters, decorating bags, tips and instructions for five exciting designs.

This stand-up guy makes a perfect centerpiece!

Polar Bear Express

For quick decorating and delightful results, our bear is hard to top! To achieve best results with upright cakes, use your favorite pound cake recipe or packaged mix for a sturdy, firm-textured cake.

Wilton Products:
3-D Cuddly Bear Pan Set
Tips 3, 17, 233
Christmas Red, Black Icing Colors

Buttercream Icing (Recipe Below)
Candy Cane, Red Licorice Twist

Bake cake according to pan directions. Trim off ears of bear. Using tip 3, pipe dot eyes, nose and outline mouth. Add tip 3 dot highlights to eyes and nose. Ice bottom of paws smooth.

Cover bear with tip 233 pull-out fur; position candy cane and over-pipe hand area. For ear muffs, position red licorice and pipe tip 17 pull-out stars to cover ears. *Serves 12.*

BUTTERCREAM ICING

½ Cup Solid Vegetable Shortening
½ Cup Butter or Margarine*
1 Teaspoon Wilton Clear
  Vanilla Extract
4 Cups Sifted Confectioners Sugar
  (approx. 1 lb.)
2 Tablespoons Milk

Cream butter and shortening with electric mixer. Add vanilla. Gradually add sugar, one cup at a time, beating well on medium speed. Scrape sides and bottom of bowl often. When all sugar has been mixed in, icing will appear dry. Add milk and beat at medium speed until ready to use. For best results, keep icing bowl in refrigerator when not in use. Refrigerated in an airtight container, this icing can be stored 2 weeks. Rewhip before using. *Makes 3 cups. For Chocolate Buttercream:* Add the following to basic recipe: ¾ cup cocoa or three 1 oz. unsweetened chocolate squares, melted, and an additional 1 to 2 tablespoons milk. Mix until well blended. *Substitute all-vegetable shortening and ½ teaspoon Wilton Butter Extract for pure white icing and stiffer consistency.

You'll find so many easy ways to serve our 3-D Cuddly Bear—iced fluffy with candy details, molded in crisped cereal mix or packed with ice cream. Look on the box for fun designs to celebrate with at showers, birthdays or holidays throughout the year.

Frosty Yule Log

Wilton Products:
10 x 15 in. Jelly Roll/Cookie Pan
Cookie Spatula
Candy Melts®*—Light Cocoa,
 Christmas Mix (1 bag each needed)
Disposable Decorating Bags

Yellow Sponge Cake
 Recipe (see below)
Buttercream, Chocolate
 Buttercream Icing Recipes, p. 91
Large Marshmallow
Confectioners Sugar

Prepare Yellow Sponge Cake recipe. Pour batter into pan, spreading evenly from center out. Tap pan several times on table to break any air bubbles. Bake in center of oven 13-15 minutes. Loosen sides. Turn out of pan onto clean kitchen towel sprinkled with 1 tablespoon granulated sugar. Remove waxed paper; roll cake and let cool, seam side down.

To Make Candy Bark: Melt Candy Melts and pour into jelly roll pan, let set at room temperature until firm enough to make candy bark using cookie spatula. Glide edge of spatula against hardened candy to create pieces of bark. Set aside.

For Pine Needles: Melt green Candy Melts in disposable bag. Cut a small hole in tip of bag and pipe lines, 3 inches long. Let set.

For Berries: Melt red Candy Melts in disposable bag. Cut a small hole in tip of bag and pipe dots for berries. Let set.

When cool, unroll cake and spread with Chocolate Buttercream Icing to within 1 in. of ends. Re-roll and place seam side down. Ice smooth with Chocolate Buttercream Icing. Position marshmallow on top center of log and ice smooth. Lighten Chocolate Buttercream with White Buttercream. Ice ends of log and top of knot with spatula to give a woodgrain spiral effect. Attach chocolate bark to log, overlapping each row. Position pine needles and berries. Sprinkle with confectioners sugar. *Makes 10 servings.*

YELLOW SPONGE CAKE RECIPE		
YELLOW SPONGE CAKE RECIPE	5 large eggs	½ teaspoon cream of tartar
	Pinch of salt	½ cup sifted granulated sugar
	¾ teaspoon vanilla	¾ cup sifted cake flour

Preheat oven to 400°F. Line jelly roll pan with waxed paper or parchment paper; lightly grease paper. Separate eggs; beat yolks 1 minute. Add pinch of salt to egg whites, beat until foamy. Add cream of tartar and continue beating whites until they cling to sides of bowl, beat 1 minute longer. Fold beaten egg yolks into egg whites gently but quickly. Fold in sugar (do not stir), flour and vanilla.

Bar cookies, made in the Wilton Jelly Roll/Cookie Pan, are excellent for "bring-a-dish" holiday parties. They travel well, serve easily and taste great.

This chocolatey treat fills the whole house with warmth!

My wife's cookies make everyone feel at home!

Mrs. Claus Welcomes You

Fondant can be shaped so easily — it's great for creating details like her puffed sleeves or scalloped apron. Try this design with your favorite pound cake or fruit cake recipe.

Wilton Products:
Wonder Mold Kit
Teen Doll Pick
Tips 1, 1s, 2, 12, 349
Red-Red, Kelly Green,
  Golden Yellow Icing Colors
Ready-To-Use Rolled Fondant
  (1 pk. needed)
Decorating Triangle
Decorator Brush Set
Florist Wire

Buttercream Icing, p. 91
Patterns (apron, collar, cuffs,
  sleeves, bodice back,
  cookie tray) starting on p. 96
Doll Glasses
  (⅞ in. size from craft store)

Style doll's hair into a bun; keep in place with florist wire. Overpipe hair with tip 1 strings. Pipe tip 1 eyebrows and lips.

Divide fondant into 4 equal parts. Tint 3 parts red, leave 1 part white. Prepare cake for rolled fondant (see fondant package directions). Before covering cake, add more body to skirt by piping tip 12 "fold" lines in buttercream. Using 14 in. circle as a guide, cut skirt from red fondant. Cut slit from side to center point. Carefully cover cake, cut away excess and smooth. Add doll pick. Cut bodice pattern from fondant and position on front and back of doll. Carefully smooth and attach with brush dipped in water.

To cover sleeves, add arm portion first, followed by sleeve puffs. Cut apron using pattern and ½ in. wide dress hem, using Decorating Triangle as pattern. Cut waistband, collar and cuffs. Attach with brush and water. (Work with one piece at a time so fondant won't dry out.)

Using buttercream icing: Decorate apron with tip 1 wavy lines. Add tip 1 dots. Edge dress and apron hem with tip 1 zigzag and beads. Add tip 349 leaves with tip 2 dots on dress and in hair.

Cut Cookie Tray Pattern from cardboard. Cover with foil. Tint remaining fondant yellow. Use tip 12 to cut out fondant "cookies". Flatten slightly with finger dipped in cornstarch. Print tip 1s message and dots. Twist white

and red fondant to form candy canes. Pipe tip 1 zigzag border on tray. Pipe tip 349 leaves and tip 2 dots in corners; add cookies. Position tray in hands. If desired, press small amount of thinned down fondant in hands to secure tray. Add glasses.

Don't forget The Wonder Mold for your holiday buffets! It's great for molded salads, ice cream treats, cheese spreads and more.

CREDITS

Creative Director........................Richard Tracy
Food Editor.............................Zella Junkin
Cake Designer..........................Steve Rocco
Senior Cake Decorator..............Susan Matusiak
Cake Decorators.......................Mary Gavenda
........................Corky Kagay
........................Nancy Suffolk Guerine
........................Darcy Simonsen
Recipe Development.................Lois Levine

Food Stylists.........................Lois Hlavak
........................Andrea Duggan
Photography.........................Kathy Sanders
Photo Assistant....................Cristin Nestor
Copy Editor.........................Jeff Shankman
Writers................................Sharon Riskin, Mary Enochs
................................Marita Seiler
Design Production...............Bullet Communications, Inc.
Production Manager............. Laura Fortin
Production Coordinator.......Mary Stahulak

Wilton products used in this book are available from your local Wilton dealer. You can also write or call:

Wilton Enterprises
Caller Service #1604
2240 West 75th St., Woodridge, IL 60517   1-630-963-7100

Patterns for Mrs. Claus Welcomes You, pg. 94-95

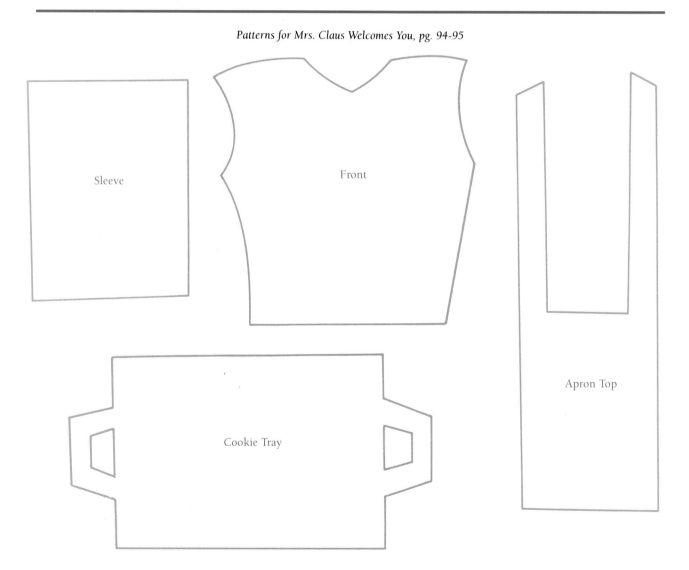